CHRISTIAN WORSHIP

Cross Cultural Theologies

Series Editors: Jione Havea and Clive Pearson, both at United Theological College, Sydney, and Charles Sturt University, Australia, and Anthony G. Reddie, Queen's Foundation for Ecumenical Theological Education, Birmingham

This series focuses on how the "cultural turn" in interdisciplinary studies has informed theology and biblical studies. It takes its leave from the experience of the flow of people from one part of the world to another.

It moves beyond the crossing of cultures in a narrow diasporic sense. It entertains perspectives that arise out of generational criticism, gender, sexual orientation, and the relationship of film to theology. It explores the sometimes competing rhetoric of multiculturalism and cross-culturalism and demonstrates a concern for the intersection of globalization and how those global flows of peoples and ideas are received and interpreted in localized settings. The series seeks to make use of a range of disciplines including the study of cross-cultural liturgy, travel, the practice of ministry and worship in multi-ethnic locations and how theologies that have arisen in one part of the world have migrated to a new location. It looks at the public nature of faith in complex, multicultural, multireligious societies and compares how diverse faiths and their theologies have responded to the same issues.

The series welcomes contributions by scholars from around the world. It includes both single-authored and multi-authored volumes.

Published:

Global Civilization
Leonardo Boff

Dramatizing Theologies: A Participative Approach to Black God-Talk
Anthony G. Reddie

Art as Theology: The Religious Transformation of Art from the Postmodern to the Medieval
Andreas Andreopoulos

Black Theology in Britain: A Reader
Edited by Michael N. Jagessar and Anthony G. Reddie

Bibles and Baedekers: Tourism, Travel, Exile and God
Michael Grimshaw

Home Away from Home: The Caribbean Diasporan Church in the Black Atlantic Tradition
Delroy A. Reid-Salmon

Working against the Grain: Black Theology in the 21ˢᵗ Century
Anthony G. Reddie

The Non-Western Jesus: Jesus as Bodhisattva, Avatara, Guru, Prophet, Ancestor or Healer?
Martien E. Brinkman
Translated by Henry and Lucy Jansen

Another World is Possible: Spiritualities and Religions of Global Darker Peoples
Edited by Dwight N. Hopkins and Marjorie Lewis

Out of Place: Doing Theology on the Crosscultural Brink
Edited by Jione Havea and Clive Pearson

Voices from the Borderland: Re-imagining Cross-cultural Urban Theology in the Twenty-first Century
Chris Shannahan

Alternatives Unincorporated: Earth Ethics from the Grassroots
George Zachariah

Forthcoming:

Towards a Systematic Spirituality of Black British Women
Marjorie Lewis

CHRISTIAN WORSHIP
POSTCOLONIAL PERSPECTIVES

Michael N. Jagessar and Stephen Burns

Routledge
Taylor & Francis Group
LONDON AND NEW YORK

First published 2011 by Equinox, an imprint of Acumen

Published 2014 by Routledge
2 Park Square, Milton Park, Abingdon, Oxon OX14 4RN
711 Third Avenue, New York, NY 10017, USA

Routledge is an imprint of the Taylor & Francis Group, an informa business

Notices
Practitioners and researchers must always rely on their own experience and
knowledge in evaluating and using any information, methods, compounds, or
experiments described herein. In using such information or methods they should
be mindful of their own safety and the safety of others, including parties for whom
they have a professional responsibility.

To the fullest extent of the law, neither the Publisher nor the authors, contributors,
or editors, assume any liability for any injury and/or damage to persons or
property as a matter of products liability, negligence or otherwise, or from any use
or operation of any methods, products, instructions, or ideas contained
in the material herein.

British Library Cataloguing-in-Publication Data

A catalogue record for this book is available from the British Library.

ISBN-13   978 1 84553 407 3   (hardback)
          978 1 84553 408 0   (paperback)
Library of Congress Cataloging-in-Publication Data

Jagessar, Michael N., 1955-
Christian worship: postcolonial perspectives / Michael N. Jagessar and Stephen
Burns.
   p. cm.—(Cross cultural theologies)
   Includes bibliographical references and index.
   ISBN 978-1-84553-407-3 (hb)—ISBN 978-1-84553-408-0 (pbk.) 1.
Liturgics. 2. Public worship. 3. Postcolonialism. 4. Christianity and
culture. I. Burns, Stephen, 1970- II. Title.
   BV178.J34 2010
   264.0089—dc22
                              2009042984

Typeset by S.J.I. Services, New Delhi

Contents

Foreword

Can postcolonial perspectives guide Christian worship away from the jaws of, or from continuing as vessels for, imperialism and militarism?

A trace of disbelief will not be a strange way to respond to the underlying assumptions in *Christian Worship: Postcolonial Perspectives*. This is because of the strong tendency to perceive postcolonial energies to be driving for critical interrogation of structures of control whereas most people of faith experience worship as attempting to order, structure, systematize and build up stability, values and lives. Christian worship and postcolonial modes of thinking are unlikely companions so attempting to relate and interweave them would be similar to putting a ceramic bowl with a clay vessel in the same sack. There is a very good chance that they will chip and crack each other (so don't try it at home).

Michael Jagessar and Stephen Burns take this risk seriously, and are unafraid of the chips and the cracks. Their courage, wise and otherwise, makes this book worthy of the attention of worshippers, regular or occasional, theologians, dogmatic or organic, cultural critics, liturgists, postcolonial critics, and so forth. Burns and Jagessar take their lead from biblical and theological critics who favour postcolonial optics, and they use those to expose and untangle the colonial agenda in Christian liturgy and worship. The upshot is a book that seeks to decolonize the soul of Christian worship by attending to a wide range of issues: conversation, tradition, service of words, festivals, bible, mission, table, hymns, language, empire, baptism, ordination and even the appeal to and misuse of Christian teachings by public and political leaders, such as Tony Blair and George W. Bush. *Christian Worship: Postcolonial Perspectives* is thus a textbook kind of volume.

Given that the colonial agenda also flows in the veins of the Christian mission, and that empire language also reverberates through Christian teachings and doctrines, all of which rely on the currents of Christian worship, the preference for postcolonial optics is necessary. This is not to say that postcolonial optics are free of blind spots, but it is unhelpful and irresponsible to avoid the conversations that Jagessar and Burns invite. It is necessary to enter those conversations for they will give us different perspectives on, at least, the powers of worship.

As a biblical critic, I especially appreciate the attention that Burns and Jagessar give to scriptures, which have been used over the centuries to fund the colonial project. Scriptures indeed live in the eyes of the public and are trimmed according to worship experiences. Cultures of hegemony, triumphalism and superiority mishandle/ sanitize scriptures by silencing their rich voices and countering perspectives. Christian worship and tradition have played significant roles in this, urged by the cultural arrogance of their gatekeepers. In this regard, *Christian Worship: Postcolonial Perspectives* is inviting space for worth-ship conversation.

In the postcolonial spirit, I point out that the scope of the book is broad but this does not mean that everything is relevant for everyone. I, for instance, am one of those who find the Festival of lessons and carols addressed in Chapter 5 foreign, but this does not mean that we have fewer worship matters to decolonize. We have our own whirlwind of traditional rituals and customs that discriminate, such as the Kava ceremonies in Oceania which exclude women and commoners. There are imperial impulses in Kava ceremonies, with dynamics of power that parallel the assumption of "being set apart" presumed in the holiness codes and in popular understandings of baptism and ordination. The place of Kava ceremonies in Christian gatherings needs to come into the scope of postcolonial optics. There are thus areas awaiting the kind of conversation, or treason, that *Christian Worship: Postcolonial Perspectives* starts. The invitation to rethink our traditions with which the book closes should therefore extend to cultural traditions outside of (traditional, Eurocentric) Christian worship. And what would Christian worship be without chips and cracks?

Jione Havea

Preface

The idea of this volume was first planted as a result of some frustration about patterns for worship and liturgical texts used in worship at Queen's Foundation for Ecumenical Theological Education, Birmingham (UK). In spite of the progressive ethos of the institution, the exciting number of diversity content modules taught at Queen's, and the constant revisions of liturgical texts, worship still often tended to remain locked into ecclesial patterns that reflected little or no engagement with the development in our academic disciplines. At Queen's we were sometimes struck by the lack of influence on worship of the insights from the various optics through which we were reading theology and texts (gendered, Black, queer, "disabled") in the classrooms. We were elated on the occasions when students and colleagues dared to step out and bring a breath of cathartic fresh air to worship. As colleagues we have been in constant conversation over these matters. Part of our ongoing conversation is represented in a collection we edited together with our colleague Nicola Slee, *The Edge of God,*[1] and if *The Edge of God* represented our enjoyment of Queen's at (in our view) its best, *Christian Worship: Postcolonial Perspectives* both extends and expands its critical questions, as they arose in an institution, however progressive, that is enmeshed in dynamics we explore here.

Stephen Burns, whose specialization is liturgy, is also a contextual theologian with interest in a breadth of contexts, and his move to Australia locates him as one of the many members of the English Diaspora. Michael Jagessar, whose initial expertise lies in systematic theology and ecumenism, will also describe himself as a "generalist" as is typical of many Caribbean scholars. Hence, his interest and engagement includes biblical hermeneutics, Black theology, the crafting of transgressing liturgical texts, and Caribbean literature. Michael is a member of the Caribbean Diaspora in England.

In our conversations we continue to wrestle with ways to interrogate inherited liturgical texts through various lenses. Needless to say, given that we have worked on this book across continents, situated in different ecclesial traditions, we have kept various contexts in mind throughout. Working in, and remembering, situations that are both different and related have no doubt shaped the tone of our work. What we offer in the following pages is an unsystematic, fragmentary, piecemeal and unfinished – and yet for us challenging, unsettling, exciting and rewarding – shared insight into numerous and ongoing conversations about the shape, style and future of Christian worship in postcolonial perspective. In doing so, we are mindful of the ways in which either one or both disciplines – postcolonial and liturgical theologies – may be unfamiliar to some readers. We are keen to note that both, it would seem, are marginal to "modern theology" as it is depicted in a collection such as David Ford's *The Modern Theologians*.[2] First published in 1989 and now in its third (2005) edition, a chapter contributed by R. S. Sugirtharajah has appeared on "postcolonial biblical criticism." Even in that third edition, postcolonial biblical criticism (notably not "theology" – itself an indicator that postcolonial perspectives have as yet concentrated on biblical study) is gathered together in the fifth part of the book with other material described as "particularizing theologies": "Black theology," "Latin American liberation theology" and "African theology," and so on. Such particularizing theologies are therefore inevitably presented as ancillary to "classics" that occupy part one. Those occupants – Barth, Bonhoeffer, Tillich, de Lubac, Rahner and von Balthasar – are, of course, all European. In this context we note also that none of the three editions of *The Modern Theologians* has included material on liturgical theology – which is odd not least given Ford's own earlier work on "theology in praise."[3]

We have written with different "audiences" very much in mind. Firstly, we have written to encourage students of Christian worship to pursue tentative interdisciplinary engagements in their subject area, urging them to bring their liturgical studies into conversation with perspectives only very rarely connected to it. So we hope that this book helps to relate what is purveyed in courses on liturgy with other aspects of the syllabus. In progressive institutions especially, there is a clear need for such work. As our experience, narrated in a following chapter, testifies, we value seminaries, and so we hope that this text is valuable not least to students in theological colleges. Secondly, we have written for persons engaged in work in postcolonial, Black and Asian and other contextual theologies. To such persons, we offer our work as an invitation and a challenge to remember the broad, overlapping, audiences of academy and church. We perceive a need for postcolonial and other contemporary theologies to attend to how their much needed insights, alternatives, challenges and subversions are manifest in Christian assembly. If our book helps in any way to "stretch" postcolonial understandings, making them available to a broader audience than other kinds of academic writing in this area, we will be happy. Thirdly, we have written for participants and presiders in Christian worship, to invite questions, directions and consideration of how liturgical theology and practice needs in certain respects, in different measures in different situations, to be chastened, expanded and re-visioned in conversation with postcolonial perspectives.

We are grateful to the community at Queen's, who make it a place where it is possible to ask questions. And our thanks are due to Janet Joyce at Equinox Press, copy-editor Sarah Norman, and the editors of the Cross Cultural Theologies series, our colleagues Jione Havea, Clive Pearson and Anthony Reddie, as well as our partners Leonora Visser 't Hooft and Judith Atkinson, for their patience and encouragement.

Garibay: *The Arrival: In His Image*

We are grateful to the artist Emmanuel Garibay for permission to reproduce his *The Arrival: In His Image*[1] both here and on the cover of this book. The image dates from 2004 and is one of many of Garibay's works critiquing colonizing Christianity, even as he himself stands within the Christian tradition from the perspective of his own Filipino optic. We note that Garibay is highly theologically trained – not least having undertaken a seminary education (after which he was never ordained). We also acknowledge that we view his work from our own particular locations, and that what his painting means to us it may not mean to him, and vice versa.

The Arrival depicts a missionary scene. A boat – evoking for us associations with conquistadores, crusades, and indeed piracy

– looms on the horizon. The scene conjures up popular imagery in Caribbean historical discourse about Columbus on his arrival ashore the pristine beach of San Salvador, accompanied by soldiers and priests. The imagery is that of a Columbus landing on the shore, planting the flag of Spain, falling on his knees thanking God and then planting that flag upon the welcoming Indians!

All three figures stand in the sea. The seascape in Garibay's work is not insignificant for us. Many postcolonial writers ascribe to the oceanic space a new symbolic dimension which challenges western tradition. As they plunge into the deep waters of a forgotten crossing, poets, for instance, come to the same conclusion that "the Sea is History," as Derek Walcott's poem puts it.[2] For us the sea conjures up imagery of fluidity that deconstructs notions of boundary, border and centre and ironically conveys a sense of belonging that significantly re-maps western notions of territory and identity. Too much of our theological articulation has been associated with the "dry land"; hence the deadliness of some of our theology. Too much of our inherited theology is premised on dogmas that supported/support expansionist and excluding policies, grounded on fixed/fossilized notions of identity, election and purity. Expansionist notions aside, can the sea and seascape provide us with notions of fluidity, ambivalence, theological ghost stories and wrecks of the deep to enable us to expunge such restrictive theology? The Caribbean writer Edward Kamau Brathwaite draws on the Caribbean sea to articulate the notions of "sub-*marine*," "sea-metrics," and the *tidalectic* nature of sea. Brathwaite suggests "tidalectic" to explore the spaces in-between or the third-space and the ebb and flow of the lives of its people.[3] The point for us is that "sea" becomes a matrix-metaphor, and looking at this picture by Emmanuel Garibay, we wonder: what can theology glean and learn from the oceanic or sea-site which serves as an in-between space (or "limbo" spaces) embodying hybridity and de-territorialization? Can this site help us to move beyond inhumanity to the celebration of cross-cultural hybridity, the discovery of fluid identities and shifting metaphors? Certainly, by evoking border-less-ness (as is associated with sea) and un-grasp-ability, oceanic images like coral, depth, tides, currents, to and fro/ebb and flow movements can provide theologians with some fresh insights to help narrate their exilic experiences, hybrid and mixed identities, and enable them to embrace their mixed identities. The cyclic paradigms, fragmentary styles and marine metaphors of many of the writers with whom we engage in this work echo the chaos of history on a subjective level. As with the past, or with the ebb and flow of the sea, neither identity, ideas, nor truth can be seized tightly. What, we wonder, does the metaphor of the sea speak to an all-too-common tendency to lock down in precise language notions of God? For the imagery of the sea itself invites our critical scrutiny of the theologies we have inherited.

Then to the figures in Gairbay's tableaux. The central figure in Garibay's painting, a White-skinned man, carries an image of a Jesus, that looks just like him, to shore. He is wading out of the water, as if in a reversal of baptism. His look of cunning, accented by the gesture of his hand that frames his face, also suggests that this encounter with water is no return to innocence. In fact, his hand makes the shape of a gun: he is deadly. Nor is his clothing a signal of any baptismal purity (which, we note in anticipation of issues we explore later in this book, is "traditionally" White). He is wearing harlequin's clothes. And the most significant piece of clothing is his headgear, for while his Jesus wears a crown of thorns, he himself sports a crown of gold, doubtless plundered.

The missionary/harlequin/king is flanked by two other figures. On his left is a brown-skinned and half-naked "native." It is significant in itself that, in an image of what we take to be her homeland, she is decentred in *The Arrival*, even though she is extending hospitality to a boatload of foreigners (note again the anchored ship in the background). If, in legend at least, Governor Arthur Phillip's first impressions of the particular male indigenous Australians that he saw were that they were "manly" (hence the name of the famous beach in Sydney), this native is evidently feminine, the contours of her body bare. And she bows in greeting, welcome or awe – bowing, we note, being a longstanding liturgical gesture associated with vulnerability: "bent over, we pause for a moment, lingering in the precariousness."[4] In any case, her posture, in this context, suggests an ambiguous obsequiousness. While there is an obvious undercurrent of both sexual allure and imbalanced power in this depiction, we think that although at first seemingly subservient, she may not in fact be so quietly compliant, and in context can be seen as embodying and "signifying" a critique not just of the missionary's religion, but potentially also of the viewer's – the art-lover's – art. For she resembles the female figures who feature in many "Tahitian" works of Paul Gauguin (note, for instance, perhaps his most famous painting in this mode, *Where Did We Come From? What Are We? Where Are We Going?* of 1897) – that late nineteenth-century French artist who, like Garibay in his own time, once attended seminary. Her role in the painting – at least, as we view it – is also to question the alliance of art, sex and power – and perhaps each in their allegiances with religion. Aside, and yet pertinent we think, it is notable that Gauguin was an artist who in his time presented images of Christ that deeply challenged his contemporaries – his *Yellow Christ* of 1889 not only planted the cross of Jesus in the local landscape of Brittany, France, where he executed the painting, but presented his Jesus un-haloed, and resembling himself – as can be seen from his *Self Portrait with Yellow Christ* of 1890–91. And Garibay in his turn is perhaps best known for his "Emmaus" series of Christa images, in which Jesus is depicted as female, literally stigmatic, and at home in a bar, drinking beer, in a vibrant and raucous environment.[5] These images are far from the green pastures, still waters, and even shadowy crosses of so many stained-glass windows. As Garibay says of his Christa, "the point is that the joke is that people are laughing because they thought all along that Jesus was a man, and that Jesus is a Caucasian looking guy ... all these conventional concepts about Jesus. I have a different image of Jesus which is that of a woman, a very ordinary looking Filipino woman, who drinks with them and has stories to tell."[6] It may or may not be that Garibay imagines the female figure in *The Arrival* as an alternative Christ/a, juxtaposed to the Jesus manhandled to shore by the king. But at the very least, there is the sense that she is the focus for grace and holiness that we see before us.

To the right of the missionary/harlequin/king, another figure stalks. He follows the king, and although not leading may be giving instruction or counsel to the one who walks before him. This figure is evidently a cleric. He wears an alb reminiscent of a religious order, such as those that led Catholic manifestations of missionary enterprise. He wears spectacles – he is, apparently, learned – perhaps a theologian?[7] He wears red, the colour of episcopal attire in Anglican choir dress, and that of cardinals in Catholic ritual: this is no sideshow of the church, but comes from the centre, or top-down, or however imaged, from a position of authority. And he is dour, sour-faced – not just White, but pasty, as if somehow sick. There is little about his face that is suggestive of "abundant life" (John 10:10), and if not indeed an anti-Christ, he is at least a converse of Dominic – founder of a Catholic missionary movement – who, according to hagiography at least, had a "joyful heart [that] animated [his] face."[8] If Dominic's hagiographers told a tall story about his cheerful animation, then the attire and face of the bishop/priest/ religious in *The Arrival* suggest that this figure is also larger than life, though in a distinctly more sinister twist than with the originator of the Order of Preachers. For this one disturbingly evokes associations with Grimm fairy-tales, if not also the mythological Grim Reaper. His face has a nose out of all proportion: so this priest is Pinocchio – a liar, the tricker's right-hand man. And his red robe might well also fit Little Red Riding Hood – so this priest is no good shepherd, but a wolf capable of devouring his prey. His advent brings death: cultural genocide, material destruction, human demise. Fairytales and myths apart, this religious figure in *The Arrival* clearly carries a processional cross – for this arrival has liturgical significance. So, with thanks to Emmanuel Garibay, we turn to our postcolonial perspectives on Christian worship.

Introduction: Context, Conversation, Critique

Context is at the heart of this project and our conversation began in a context laced with multiple layers and meanings. One of the first things that greets visitors upon entering the dining room, the largest gathering space in the Queen's Foundation for Ecumenical Theological Education (also known as Queen's College),[1] is the imposing portrait of a young Queen Victoria, shoulders fully exposed. The image is of no Queen in mourning – and in a number of ways the portrait links the institution to a colonial past, as Britain's colonial history is also tied to Victoria's and Britannia's ruling of the waves. Yet, ironically, the Queen's College has been one of the theological "spaces" in the UK that has (both intentionally and unintentionally) offered critique and alternatives to colonial and imperial theology. Over the years, Queen's has been one of the most progressive institutions for theological education and ministerial formation for the churches in the UK, in terms of the diversity of its staff and the content of some of the courses designed and taught.[2]

In highlighting Victoria's portrait, the point to stress is that there is considerable complexity to the context from which this work has evolved. Queen's is located in the leafy suburb of Edgbaston, in which much of the land is still owned by the Calthorpe family – a clear reminder of class and landowning families. The progeny of colonization's children, within a short bus-ride to majority multicultural communities, populate the surrounding areas, though almost nowhere in the city is as leafy as Farquhar Road on which Queen's is situated. Yet, at Queen's itself, the student body remains predominantly White though there has been some shift in terms of ethnicities from both global and local British contexts. Even so, persons from ethnic minorities are still marginal as Queen's still struggles to attract Black-British and Asian-British candidates for the church's ministry. Students and staff are from the Church of England, Methodist, and

United Reformed ecclesial traditions. During our time and more recently, students from younger ecclesial traditions such as the Metropolitan Christian Community and Black Majority Pentecostal churches have been joining the college community and the large body of independent students.

We have had to wrestle with why, in spite of the history, the exposure and opportunities at Queen's, it remains that oftentimes little change in liturgical theology and practice is evidenced among students. This forced us to reflect more deeply on our curriculum and what we were teaching in our particular areas. As colleagues, we have had numerous opportunities to share our joys, pains, frustrations and challenges in teaching, wrestling with the treasures of our respective ecclesial traditions and participating in the formation of public ministers. We quickly noted what has become one of our deepest convictions, that while significant, cutting-edge and diversity content courses may be taught, all to the good, there remains the need for a deeper conversation *across* disciplines that will impact on what we teach and how and what students engage with and learn and will put into practice. Consequently, we have had many conversations around how liturgical theology and practice engages with courses such as Black, Asian and feminist theologies, postcolonial studies and the other optics. We have become aware, as Musa Dube rightly observes, that there is still the need to decolonize the curriculum in theological education. Indeed, much of our programmes are still "circumscribed by colonial boundaries."[3] Interestingly, we are yet to read or to hear any reflections on the role of "Queen" in "Queen's Foundation," which is, in some way, related to R. S. Sugirtharajah's point that theologians in the West/Europe are yet to reflect on "European expansionism and the rise of their own discipline" or "to offer a sustained theological analysis of the impact of colonialism."[4]

Consequently, as colleagues whose heart and work are in specific disciples (contextual and liberation theologies, ecumenism, liturgy and interfaith studies) and at the same time adventurous enough to transgress disciplines and interest (Caribbean literature, postcolonial hermeneutics, and Black theology) our conversation has led to our investigation of the lack of any attempt to relate liturgy and postcolonialism – the specific brief of this book.

The relationship between liturgical studies and postcolonial criticism is not a present concern for scholars in these distinct strands of scholarly inquiry. In fact, liturgical studies and postcolonial criticism – like so many other fields – are oftentimes treated as separate strands of the wider theological enterprise. To date, biblical scholars have engaged with postcolonial criticism in a more fulsome way than other colleagues in theological study, but we find it especially strange (though not surprising) that liturgical studies and postcolonial criticism have remained almost entirely disconnected, given the central place of liturgy and worship to the Christian belief, and to the missionary and the colonial agenda.

One early response to this dearth has been our groundbreaking article "Fragments of a Postcolonial Perspective on Christian Worship" (published in the leading North American journal of liturgical theology, *Worship*, in 2006, and in revised form in *Black Theology: An International Journal* in 2007). This was a first attempt to sketch out the contours of a conversation between the two disciplines, and it has stirred our own and others' curiosity about how such a conversation might be extended. We have also included that essay in this collection where it belongs. *Christian Worship: Postcolonial Perspectives* develops our ideas into a short book that surveys the terrain of liturgical theology through sustained postcolonial optics: it continues that conversation and sketches out areas for ongoing attention. Integral to this scrutiny are the cross-cultural and intercultural perspectives on theology and liturgy. We observe, however, that there is within the discourse on postcolonial criticism the tendency for this to remain within the academic realm. This is noticeably so in terms of biblical studies and more recently in theological discourse where these ideas are yet to reach congregational contexts. What our engagement through worship offers is an opportunity and a potential means to facilitate the postcolonial optic reaching the gathered community via the conversation with liturgy. As such, a postcolonial engagement with Christian worship allows postcolonial insights to reach a broader "public."

At the heart of this project is the word "conversation." If there is a paradigm or a metaphor to describe our journey to this point, "conversation" is it. We are mindful that the word "conversation" in Latin means "an act of living with" or "keeping company with" or "turn about with." Then sometime in the late eighteenth century, it became a legal term for adultery, having evolved from being a synonym for sexual intercourse. All of the meanings point to an intimate act that intends to transgress closed boundaries.

Yet we not only engage in conversations; we *are* a conversation. Human persons are hybrid, hyphenated, sometimes contradictory, searching, unreconciled, and ever complex entities. The voice we bring to the conversation is heavily shaped by our heritages, facets of our socialization processes and cultures. Yet voicing conversations is certainly ideological and will reflect how and where we position ourselves. As Diana Eck notes, voice or voicing "depends upon the location of people to [and with] whom we speak, the context in which we speak, and what is at stake in that context."[5] This makes it plain that voicing a conversation that is dialogical, such as ours, is not without tension and challenges. We are aware of this, as we are aware of the positive fruits of such a commitment. There is also much to be said about friendship that becomes a habit, a context and a safe space in which we are able to converse by asking critical questions and inviting scrutiny of each others' perspective and traditions.

With this understanding we hope that our conversations can engender a capacity to move *beyond* just "good intentions."[6] Here *beyond* is a minor word with major possibilities, especially given Homi Bhabha's use of the term in the context of postcolonialism. Bhabha reads *beyond* as that which "signifies spatial distance, marks progress, promises the future," mindful that "the very act of going *beyond*" takes us into the "unknowable, un-representable, without a return to the 'present', which, in the process of repetition, becomes disjunct and displaced."[7] *Beyond* also underscores "its hope to transcend its shortcomings."[8] Bhabha's insight that *beyond* opens up both an "intervening space," and a "revisionary time" ripe with transforming empowering possibilities for the present, is at the heart of our endeavour.

Further, we represent different disciplines and yet are interested in each other's work. This kind of a conversation enables something to happen that neither of us could quite manage on our own. We are moved *beyond* our own limitations fully aware of the dangers of re-inscribing that which we seek to scrutinize. Thus "conversation" here becomes an epistemological habit we want to embody and engender through this work. This demands attentiveness to each other, to scholars and colleagues and to traditions, as *beyond* implies that we offer provisional thoughts and insights that may provide questions and vistas for an ongoing discourse. Postcolonialism forces us not only to affirm diversity and resist totalizing proclivities, but to also recognize the partial and limited nature of our findings. These cannot be locked into exactitudes.

Consequently, attentiveness cannot be separated from criticality: bringing to the fore a degree of assertiveness. Moving *beyond* "good intentions" necessarily demands critical assertiveness and a spirit of openness. From a postcolonial perspective, there is much to critique in the study of liturgy and the celebration of Christian worship. Throughout the book, we will point to some of the different dimensions that need to be scrutinized and thought through afresh. The crucial question for us relates to the challenge of handling and negotiating the weight that tradition carries in the construction of what passes as acceptable worship or worship that is affirmed in liturgical theology. We are aware that this will require careful self-scrutiny on our part as we also inhabit some of these traditions. In this regard, we draw wisdom from Gordon Lathrop's insight on the task of contemporary liturgical theology as "critical classicism."[9] How do we negotiate both openness to the tradition and a commitment to subject it to questions in the light of colonial, postcolonial and contemporary concerns?

We are acutely aware of the tendency to affirm the capacity of tradition itself to act as a critical voice (or a cacophony of critical voices) that can punch at contemporary perspectives to which persons might otherwise become captive to (or tunnel-visioned by) the merely contemporary. We are also aware that we will need to reconsider our assumptions about tradition. Even the good things about tradition – the capacity to critique the narrowly contemporary – need to be subject to some forceful basic questions, most notably for instance, "what do we mean by tradition" and "*whose* tradition"? Questions about how traditions other than those that came to be dominant might be heard or reconstructed, and how prevailing traditions need to be decentred and relativized, will have deep consequences for whatever notion of "critical classicism" remains possible – if that notion can or ought to survive at all.

Here we have found helpful the lexicology of the word "tradition" (in Latin) which not only means to deliver, surrender, transmit or handover. It also means "treason," that is, to hand someone over to the enemy by fraud. There is clearly a relationship between tradition and treason, with Massimo Leone suggesting that "treason, which prospers, is called tradition."[10] It is our hope that what we have to offer in these pages would engender treason that prospers – handing over, but not necessarily prescribing and bringing closure on insights.

Shape of the Chapters/Texts

Following these introductory comments, the book is divided into five parts. The first explains our option for a particular (postcolonial) optic, telling stories that locate us (the authors), acknowledging our different and related perspectives, exposing some of our subjectivities, and encouraging readers to reflect upon their own. We also introduce some of the key features of postcolonial theology, some of which we will re-engage with, apply and elaborate throughout the sections of this volume. We also review a selection of significant works in liturgical studies, noting the absence of postcolonial perspectives. The first Part clearly establishes the interdisciplinary nature of our study and sets the framework for the particular trajectories we explore in more detail in each of the subsequent chapters.

In Part Two, "The Mixed Media of Liturgy," we focus on two key themes: "Liturgical Texts and Symbolic Contexts" and "Embodying Theology in Song." In the former we propose to explore some key postcolonial challenges to various dimensions of Christian worship, opening up conversation through special reference to images of light and darkness in key texts and symbols of the "classical" western liturgical tradition. Recognizing that many Protestant and Pentecostal Christians learn theology especially through the medium of song, the latter theme surveys the ambiguous legacy of Christian hymnody as well as identifying postcolonial concerns for the attention of contemporary hymn-writers, hymnal compilers and congregational musicians.

Having given space to various media comprising Christian worship, Part Three, "The Word in Liturgical Contexts," attends to one particular medium that is shared across almost every Christian tradition: the public reading of the Bible. It engages the growing literature on postcolonial biblical criticism and enlarges that discourse to encircle both church and academy by explicitly focusing on use of the Bible as the churches' scriptures. As part of this, the chapter critiques the dynamics of ecumenical lectionaries and considers strategies for enacting the postcolonial tactic of contrapuntal reading in liturgical contexts.

Part Four comprises reflections on Time, Space and Persons. Firstly, we focus on deconstructing a specific event in the calendar of some churches that is closely associated with a particular place, and which some suppose to be "quintessentially English": the Christmas Eve office of readings broadcast worldwide by King's College, Cambridge. This study integrates material earlier in the book on scripture, symbol and song to develop some key features of a postcolonial understanding of liturgical time; by exploring the development of this service in one particular location, it also introduces a range of considerations for postcolonial scrutiny of liturgical space. The latter theme scrutinizes the Church of England's recent *Common Worship: Initiation Services* and *Common Worship: Ordination Services* alongside parallel material in other ritual books, and explores and critiques ways in which these liturgies purport to construct identities, self-consciousness and perception of others. Like Chapter 5, this chapter applies a focused postcolonial gaze upon particular trajectories of Christian worship, and offers illustrative examples of how such an optic can be turned to survey and critique inherited and assumed worship practices. These two foci contribute strongly to the "practical" character we desire for our study. This chapter then concludes with reflections on modest attempts to decolonize curricula in liturgical studies for those who come to participate and preside in liturgies, not least baptism and ordination.

Finally, a concluding reflection offers some threads to the discourse we have carried out in our study and exploration of postcolonial perspectives on Christian worship. By centring on the notion of tradition – its authority, ambiguity and resourcefulness – we hope to concentrate our key convictions and highlight concerns and trajectories for further attention by ourselves and most importantly, we hope, by other colleagues. In our view, this is work in progress and part of a lifetime's learning.

Part One

Postcolonial Optics

1 On Opting for an Optic

The term "postcolonial" is contested, is put to different uses by different persons, and shelters a range of distinct, though related, convictions, methods and themes. Postcolonial theology has begun to elaborate on this cluster of issues in relation to texts and doctrines, and our own present work is an attempt to expand attention from texts and doctrines to symbols and practices that shape Christian assembly, in what we believe to be a distinctive initiative. By examining the diverse ways in which the term postcolonial is used, we enlarge some understandings more widely held in common: that postcolonial perspectives involve (i) affirmation of the equal dignity of human beings, (ii) exposure of imperial dynamics at play in culture and politics, unreflective everyday practices as well as carefully and intentionally constructed policies, and (iii) celebration of subaltern wisdom, creativity and resistance to dominant supposed "norms." The liturgical genres that provide counterparts for these foci are perhaps bold proclamation, searching lament and generous praise. And perhaps the convergence of postcolonial and liturgical concerns also beckons, or provokes, an invitation to repentance?

We offer further biographical material in the course of our reflections, but at the outset state that one of us is Black, an Indo-Guyanese person who currently resides in the UK and whose familial commitments also link him to mainland Europe and North America. The other is White, a British person who currently resides in Australia, whose familial commitments link him to sojourners in North America and Asia as well as indigenous Australia. Both have some, though very different, experiences of Diaspora. One's teaching and published work is closely identified with "Black theology," being the reviews editor of an international journal that bears that name and having published two books with the phrase "Black theology" in the title line, one of which also bears the descriptor "postcolonial." The other is closely associated with studies of "liturgy" and "worship," marked by critical classicist approaches and often of an inter-disciplinary nature. This makes our partnership in this joint exploration of postcolonial perspectives of Christian worship both appropriate and strong, and expands our previous joint writing on the convergence of our concerns, and our joint editing with another colleague, Nicola Slee, of a collection that includes alongside our own contributions a number of others' postcolonial perspectives on liturgical topics.

Still, we are not without reserve in pursuing this project. Firstly, we cannot possibly provide anything like a comprehensive postcolonial critique of liturgical tradition and practice. We do not attempt to revisit the kind of introduction to liturgical studies that one of us has written but this time more intentionally through postcolonial optics. Rather, we must settle instead for something more piecemeal and modest that nevertheless suggests the challenging implications of this approach for liturgical foci we are unable to unfold here. More than that, however, our reserve – and particularly, perhaps that of Stephen Burns – is about the possibility, let alone appropriateness, of a White person addressing the concerns that emerge in this book. We affirm that "White liberals" (such as Stephen imagines others as well as himself might assume himself to be) – and moreover White persons in general – need to be confronted with postcolonial perspectives. We submit that White persons who attempt to voice postcolonial perspectives are rightly vulnerable to possible charges of paternalism and the oftentimes gross attempt to speak for another, such as one should not and indeed in fact cannot. Still, we tentatively wish to suggest that the risks of a White person attempting to give voice to postcolonial perspectives are at least reduced by our method in which we both jointly own the convictions in this book, as we together embrace a revisionist agenda for Christian worship. Further, we also hold the view that as the progenies of both colonized and colonizer histories, the complex interrelationship forces us together. Whatever the caveats, Caliban and Prospero are inseparable (as is the significant role of Miranda) in this conversation.

Notwithstanding, our shared intent is to suggest ways in which Christian worship, as both enacted and studied, should change in response to postcolonial critique. To put it bluntly, we are committed to change rather than to silence,[1] and so we invite readers who may relate to a White liberal dilemma that should rightly be of concern also to "stutter"[2] towards speech in the conviction that change is necessary and that silence is not an option for us if it colludes with further practice of imperialism. Resort to silence can be an abrogation of integrity and responsibility.

Even so, we remain aware that as the term "liberation" has, in Rasiah Sugirtharajah's term, been "highjacked,"[3] so there is a clear potential threat that postcolonial convictions and themes will be "co-opted by the Christian mainstream."[4] Sugitharajah complains of the way in which the basic tenets of liberation theology have been absorbed by theologians far from the contexts in which liberation theology emerged, and then "recast as apolitical and personal empowerment."[5] We assert that constant self-critical vigilance is required of White liberals to temper the absorption of postcolonial perspectives simply as an "enrichment" to what are undoubtedly important emancipatory but nevertheless somewhat other agendas, be they feminist, queer or whatever in their trajectory (we name these two in particular because of their prominence alongside postcolonial perspectives in our previously mentioned edited collection). We suggest that a commitment to postcolonial perspectives will involve vigilance about attempting to retain a focus on issues of ethnicity, however helpful it also is to foster the kind of bi-focal, tri-focal, and other alliances that resist the atomization of optics oftentimes regarded as "marginal." Indeed, alliance may be crucial to effective resistance of dynamics of marginalization which may more easily take place when related though distinct optics remain atomized.[6] This is to say at least that White liberal consideration – and celebration – of postcolonial perspectives needs to quite consciously and constantly be checked by reference to a tradition of postcolonial thinking which began and continues to focus on issues of ethnicity, complex and diverse as that vibrant tradition has become.

These reflections raise questions in their turn about how we relate in this work to liturgical tradition, and what might be signalled by talk (employed above) of critical classicism in relation to it. We conclude this book with reflections in this area; in the meantime, however, we note that Stephen Burns especially broadly concurs with Gordon Lathrop, who writes of being: "marked by the willing reception of traditional patterns and archaic symbols, in the belief that these classics bear authority among us ... [yet] at the same time

… marked by the willing elaboration of a contemporary critique of received tradition."[7] Together, we affirm that our explorations are committed to maintaining a focus on the ambiguities of tradition. And we assert that commitment to tradition implies commitment to "search for lost coins" within it, to echo a feminist image which has been of special importance to Stephen Burns,[8] which is essentially a constructive task.

Locating and Interrogating Selves

One of the implications of contextual theology is that it involves autobiography. We affirm Dolores Williams's sense that

> I have come to believe that theologians, in their attempt to talk to and about religious communities, ought to give readers some sense of their autobiographies. This can help an audience discern what leads the theologian to do the kind of theology she does. What has been the character of her faith journey? What lessons has this journey taught? What kind of faith inspires her to continue writing and rewriting, living and reliving theology in a highly secular Black-and-White world paying little or no attention to what theologians are saying?[9]

Conversation cannot happen in a vacuum. We are embodied and located cultural beings. We need to locate ourselves and key aspects of our stories that will have a bearing on this project. We are mindful that individual identities are multilayered, multivocal and will comprise of a complex list of descriptors. Like Geertz's "thick descriptions," there are layers upon layers that we negotiate and appropriate accordingly and conveniently. We are all plural beings whether we realize it or not. And while we may be like all others and some others; we are also like no other. We are each unique.[10]

Michael Jagessar is a progeny of the history of colonial indentureship or modified slavery of Indians from the subcontinent. He was born as a colonial subject. He grew up in a context where his grandparents, parents and siblings on both sides are still practising Hindus, Christians and Muslims. Religion was certainly the most observable fact of daily life as religious diversity was a given in that very plural community in Guyana. Michael has inherited an interfaith life with all the extras that come with the blessings of multiple religious heritages. It was natural to follow one grandparent and her Hindu rituals of morning pujas (prayers), another to church (Black step-grandfather), and yet another (maternal) to the Mosque or for midday prayers if they were in the rice fields.

While Michael's entry point into this conversation is that of a Caribbean Christian theologian, his is also a heritage heavily shaped by both Muslim and Hindu influences.[11] He breathes and lives a life of perpetual internal dialogue. As one whose life has been shaped in the Caribbean, Michael's theology, theologizing and hermeneutics reflect Caribbean impulses – especially its rainbow nature embracing a diversity of peoples, religions, cultures and the ongoing dialogue and interaction in this context, albeit in the wider Caribbean Diaspora as he is now located in Birmingham (UK).

"Marginality" may be one of the better descriptors to explain his journey thus far. Here Michael is also keen to refer to the notion of "limbonality" to embrace his multiple worlds and the ability to be located in-between two or three, in all three or beyond all, noting that it is the in-between spaces where he finds the real stuff of theologizing. This is one of the reasons why he finds it difficult to theologize with a view. His proclivity is to do theology from a multiplicity of views in creative and dynamic dialogue and tension. This is important to note as Michael has no interest in defending or articulating fossilized/monolithic theological notions. God-talk (theology) for him, especially in the context of worship and liturgy (our focus) is done through the influence of the rich world of Caribbean diversity, contradictions, ambivalence and the exciting possibilities and gateways this offers. Thus, while Michael writes from a Christian perspective, it is neither "normative" nor is it sympathetic to Euro-centric views.

Michael's spirituality is shaped by these multiple religious heritages. His transition to Christianity occurred in the context of a Lutheran School in Guyana and it is in this ecclesial tradition that he was called to ministry, attended an ecumenical seminary and was ordained. He later worked in different parts of the Caribbean (Jamaica, Grenada, Curacao) and in other ecclesial traditions (Churches of Christ, Moravian, Methodist, Presbyterian, United Protestant) before he moved to the UK (with the United Reformed Church). In all of these contexts, Michael has been and is presently involved in theological education, practice of ministry, doing theology in the context of social justice engagement, community development, and raising critical questions in these and other areas. Significant has been Michael's navigating of what he calls "wider and hybrid ecumenism" and in his teaching and writing he has constantly drawn from, challenged and critiqued these treasures and multiple blessings.

Michael contends that ecclesial and religious traditions are yet to find a theology to touch and embrace people like himself – travellers, not cemented long-term boarders.[12] The journey allows him to get to places he cannot fully figure out. Most of the time, he is stranded somewhere between origin and destination. He often moves backward, forward, outside and to a third space or in-between spaces simultaneously in his border-crossing journeys, unable to return to the same place. For Michael, two metaphors stand out: that of a dancer savouring transitional moments and a musician striving to discern and handle pauses between the notes, experiencing the Divine in the in-between spaces.[13]

Michael's academic journey has been and continues to be a movement between various worldviews and the complicated colonial history of Caribbean indenturedship that has given rise to the complexity of his story. While his "formal" theological formation took place in Guyana, Jamaica, and in the Netherlands, the wider contexts of the Caribbean have played a significant role in the shaping of his theological views. And one significant voice (among the many others) that has been influential is that of Philip Potter.[14] Michael's engagement in Caribbean literature and theology was the result of the urgings of Potter who was his MA mentor in Jamaica. It was no surprise therefore that Michael's PhD work was on Philip Potter and especially his contribution on the ecumenical scene around the dialogue of cultures.

Michael's employment of the postcolonial optic is related to this multiple and complex Caribbean heritage. This is not to claim that Michael was aware of such an optic though his thinking was and is constantly evolving. What he contends is that while it is unnamed this habit has been there long before the present theorizing. Michael's own interest in theology and Caribbean literature through his MA work in 1987 and with specific reference to writers such as C. L. R. James, Wilson Harris, Derek Walcott, Frantz Fanon, Olive

Senior, John Agard, and Edouard Glissant (among others) meant that the postcolonial optic was already taking shape in his work and writings. This is especially reflected in his later re-writing of liturgies, employment of Anansi (the Caribbean Patron saint) as conversation partner in theological discourse, his interpreting of texts and his eclectic and interdisciplinary approach to doing theology. After all, as Michael declares, the Caribbean has been the first modern multi-cultural site or experiment initiated by European colonial powers in its geopolitical, cultural, religious and economic race of empire building and Michael is ideally located to use the influences of this context, in conversation with a colleague (Stephen) from the former "mother" country, to interrogate Christian worship. Michael feels that he met an expansive generosity in Stephen that has provided a very constructive context for a fruitful conversation where the respect, integrity, mutual sharing and critical engagement with each other's ideas and that of the ecclesial traditions has been rewarding. Coming from different ends or points on a bridge of our meeting or crossing, the points where we have met have not been the places where we stopped. The adventure is too exciting and fluid for such.

Stephen Burns is a White English man, who grew up in west Cumbria, in north-west England. His earliest years were spent in a particular kind of Christian fundamentalist community, the Christian Brethren. Within the context of a study of Christian worship, it should be noted that as well as holding quirky views of biblical interpre-tation, and eschewing notions of sacramentality, the Brethren reject anything resembling an ordained ministry, and they can be trenchantly opposed to ecumenical gestures. Their identity is maintained by sustained rhetoric concerned with defining themselves against other Christians (who may not be regarded as such). The Brethren should not, however, be regarded as "non-liturgical" and their patterns of worship often conform to a very narrow repertoire much more rigid than is often found in worship in self-consciously liturgical traditions, although this is a point they may not appreciate.

The west coast of Cumbria, on which Stephen grew up, was ethnically mono-cultural, and in this regard to this day has changed little, as extensive recent studies in Lancaster University's "Kendal Project," published in part as *The Spiritual Revolution*,[15] show is the case for a nearby area. Hence, Stephen recalls no persons of an ethnic minority ever attending Brethren meetings, let alone there being any Black or Asian preachers or leaders of particular events. In his memory, persons of ethnic minorities were present in Brethren meetings only in stories mediated by visiting (invariably White) missionaries; and, notably, these missionaries were oftentimes of a particular intense outlook associated with New Tribes Mission, whose evangelistic practices enacted the dispensationism associated with one of the key figures of early Brethren tradition, James Darby, in an aggressive, not to say disturbing, way.

As a teenager, Stephen's ecclesial allegiances shifted to the Anglican tradition, in which he found greater hospitality to his questions and to the ministry of women, although the kind of Anglicanism he found was also of a rather conservative kind (despite it not seeming that way after experience of the Brethren, of course...). And, while still growing up on the edge of Cumbria, his cultural context remained much the same as in his earlier childhood. While racist attitudes were certainly embedded in the missionary activity that was lauded in church, the fact that he remembers no overt racist comment in the churches he attended is probably due to the fact that representatives of any kind of ethnic otherness were simply not present in person. In any case, overt racist comment was a frequent mark of the wider environment in which he grew up.

Over time, Stephen has shifted considerably from the theological understandings accessible to him when he was young. During his university years in Durham, encounter with feminist theologies – particularly as mediated by Ann Loades, who later became his doctoral supervisor – was very important in terms of opening up new trajectories of approach towards and understanding of the Christian tradition in its resourceful diversity. Stephen continues to credit feminist theology for sensitizing him to a range of liberation theologies, including Black and Asian theologies of different kinds. This is to say that, at least in his case, one means of contesting assumed theological understandings, and the weight of historical and contemporary consensus, evoked concern to learn from other undervalued and marginalized perspectives.

During training for ordination (and, at the same time, marriage to a woman also training to be a priest), Stephen's interest in practical theologies deepened. He remembers his postgraduate work in pastoral theology as being especially marked by a desire to deconstruct approaches to the faith he had absorbed from childhood. If this had started to happen in his initial engagement with feminist theology, it was considerably developed in sustained work to apply pastoral theological methodologies in his attempt to find an approach and understanding of his own. Through exploration of these methodologies, he was able to enact the scrutiny of his inherited faith that feminist theology had awakened and taught him to keep seeking. His inter-disciplinary postgraduate studies in Durham and Cambridge involved what he now considers a "demolishing" of the practice of forgiveness, and its associated Christian doctrines, with very few constructive proposals in view by way of response to the identification of a range of problems with the theological perspectives he surveyed.[16] Given that he was especially concerned to reflect on the abuse of children, it was no doubt inevitable that problems of theological rhetoric would be foregrounded. Stephen does not feel that his theological convictions have since become more ordered, or less piecemeal, than in this phase of his life. A sense of the ambiguity of Christian symbols and discourse is one of the abiding marks of these studies on the theological convictions he has since mustered.

Several years practising ministry as an ordained priest (in the diocese of Durham) shaped him in their own way. It was only during this period that Stephen became intensely interested in liturgical theology, the area in which his subsequent research and publishing have concentrated. In his early years of ordained priesthood, he was struck both by the importance of attendance at liturgy to members of congregations he tried to serve, as well as the sometimes rather scant interest such persons expressed about participation in certain aspects of the liturgy. That the rather narrow sacramentalism – by no means Brethren-esque, but in some respects not much broader – of persons "in the pews" was out-of-kilter with luminous ideas about the liturgy expressed in liturgical theology, particularly in some of its North American modes, where emphasis in liturgical study is not so much or only on history of the liturgy (in at least almost all of what Stephen had encountered of liturgical study in the UK), but more on its intrinsic and implied theology. This disjuncture led Stephen to study the literature on liturgical change and revision arising from the Church of England, of which by now he was of course a minister, alongside the articulate and aspirational perspectives of North American liturgical theologians such as Gordon Lathrop, Gail Ramshaw and Don Saliers.[17] Perhaps on the one hand he found within liturgical theology an emphasis on the communal context of expressed belief which would, as it were, carry his own questions and reserve about aspects of the Christian tradition. On the other hand, his explorations in liturgical theology evoked a hope that the practice of Christian worship might depict and manifest the divine reign in such a way as is attractive and at least at times accessible for persons in the parishes to which he belonged. It is, however, important to him to underscore that he does not perceive the doxological nature of liturgical theology to be a retreat from the challenges of feminist and practical theologies. Significantly, the interdisciplinary concerns that marked his earlier concentration on practical theologies have continued to mark Stephen's academic interests. Indeed, current energy expended on postcolonial scrutiny of the liturgy is one response to his suggestion of a number of much needed interdisciplinary engagements with liturgical theology, just as others – between, for example, theologies of disability, queer theologies, and the unfolding developments of feminist theology – are ones that he is also currently attempting to further.

Two other fragments from this phase of life are particularly important in the present context. One is that during his years as a full-time parish priest, Stephen made the first of several visits to Australia, where a family member had married an Aboriginal person and now lived in an inland indigenous community. This led to the beginnings of an awareness of the legacy of one very particular form of British colonialism. As one who is now resident in Australia, Stephen oftentimes finds that his relatively limited experience of contemporary Aboriginal Australia is greater, sometimes significantly so, than that of many of the White Australians he meets. While at work full-time as a priest in parish ministry, Stephen was based in a so-called "urban deprivation area," in Gateshead, north-east England, where an influx of asylum seekers and refugees were dispersed according to Home Office policy within a very short space of time around the turn of the millennium. Engagement with this widely diverse, sometimes still traumatized, and certainly very often shockingly inadequately provided-for sector of the population in many ways changed the shape of his ministry, involving not least much more intentional involvements in both local political issues and interfaith activity.[18]

Stephen had been a student in theology departments in the UK, engaged in either undergraduate or postgraduate study, for at least eight years when he was appointed as Tutor in Liturgy at the Queen's Foundation.[19] He does not recall once in all those years hearing of the notion of postcolonial criticism, let alone its relevance to theology. Of course, Stephen's studies had been concentrated in pastoral and liturgical theologies, which had at that time been almost entirely devoid of engagement with postcolonial concerns. But not much may have changed in others' experience in the intervening years, given that postcolonial criticism remains overwhelmingly engaged with biblical studies, in so far as it is taken seriously in theology at all. This notwithstanding, in Stephen's experience, working closely with Michael Jagessar revealed Stephen's unfamiliarity with postcolonial theology and its many possible theological applications, not least to the situations he had confronted in his recent experience of parish ministry. And notably, Stephen remembers co-teaching with Michael as being the first occasions in which he had himself been taught theology by a Black theologian (as opposed to reading, or reading about, Black theologians), and leading worship with Michael as among the first times he did so with persons from ethnic minorities (and likewise with colleagues Anthony Reddie, a British Methodist of Caribbean heritage, and Mukti Barton, an Asian Anglican). As suggested above, what was by this time a close familiarity with feminist theology enabled Stephen at least to begin to appreciate the importance of postcolonial theology, as well as having taught him some attitudes that (he hopes) helped him to listen. Hence, Stephen began to pick up some aspects of Michael's postcolonial optic, and subsequently their conversation frequently turned to the question of colonization in their classrooms, as well as the chapel.

For Stephen, the opportunity of co-writing this book is a conscious attempt to keep learning how postcolonial optics critique his inherited and assumed theology and practice, and not least his convictions about and practices in liturgical celebration. This is to claim neither that in the present co-written work Stephen is the sole repository of liturgical understanding – this is evidently not the case when working in partnership with Michael Jagessar – nor that Stephen is still entirely "green" in articulating postcolonial theological perspectives. For several years, he has endeavoured to do so in the contexts where he has worked, and in relation to communal and managerial decision-making, worship practices, teaching curriculum, and the wider context of ministerial formation in which these are set. It is, however, to suggest what he takes to be a proper and appropriate receptivity to the more sharply perceived force of Michael's developed and articulate perceptions about colonial and postcolonial dynamics. And it is to attempt not only passively to abandon, but actively to expunge, the traces of colonial superiority which mark Stephen's context and experience, however faintly he might feel and however much he might wish to disassociate himself from the colonizing arrogance of his history, sub-cultures and unconscious.

The Postcolonial Optic

We have already briefly hinted at our employment of a postcolonial optic in this project. In the context of colonial history and the role of Great Britain in European expansionist agenda, empire, Christianity, church and mission have been deeply involved and implicated in the oppression of colonies and their inhabitants. Mission, church and empire are closely related as are the destinies of colonized (Caliban) and colonizer (Prospero). In terms of the "civilizing" project, worship, as part and parcel of mission and church, is not value free. Kwok Pui-lan underscores the role of a common liturgy in the ethos of Anglicanism and its colonial overtones. She writes:

> Since the BCP [Book of Common Prayer] serves as a "grammar" to understand the language and religious practices of Anglicanism, it is important to analyze the cultural and linguistic world created by it.[20]

She particularly notes those "images of king and empire" that lace "the liturgy, canticles and hymns" of the BCP, as well as "imageries of light and darkness" that can "marginalize dark-skinned people and create false racial stereotypes." She goes on to suggest "that it is not enough" "to translate the BCP into local languages, without a radical examination of the book's cultural and linguistic world."[21] This is a critique that we address in the sections that follow.

So, "what is postcolonialism?" and "what does it has to do with worship and theology and practice of worship?" become important questions in the light of our undertaking. Words have considerable power and if there is a politics of locations, so there is also a politics of terminology. It is, therefore, imperative that we define what we mean by postcolonial (mindful of our own locations) and how we are going to employ this optic in scrutinizing "Christian worship." What Kwok's insight implies is the fact that theology or God-talk does not emerge *ex nihilo*. It "develops in constant negotiation with political and ecclesial empires and with other power dynamics throughout history."[22] What we have inherited in terms of Bible, tradition, reason and experience certainly needs critical evaluation. Thus, Kwok notes that these four categories

> have been defined in the past through the lens of Western culture alone. Today, they must be subject to a postcolonial scrutiny and amplified by the cultural resources from many parts of the [Anglican] Communion.[23]

What postcolonial advocates insist on is that any discourse on the Christian faith must reckon with empire and the complex relationship of church and empire.[24] As we have earlier intimated, the theorizing on and practice of Christian worship gives little or no attention to this relationship. The relationship between imperial realities and the theology of Christian worship has been largely neglected. The consequence has been impoverishment and distortion of diversity within the Christian family. The task, therefore, is both analytical and constructive with the latter depending on the former. As Joerg Rieger notes:

> Without understanding how we are shaped by empire all the way into our deeper desires, we cannot properly identify the theological surplus, those intuitions and insights that point us beyond the horizons of empire… Without the analytical exploration of theology and empire we will not be able to identify what is really path-breaking in theology, what it is that has the potential to shape truly fresh and constructive thinking about God and the world.[25]

Like other scholars, we are both aware of how the Anglo/Euro-centric domination of worship and liturgy refused and continues to refuse colonial and postcolonial territories the right to their own identities, much less their own liturgies. This is so ingrained in the Caribbean, for instance, that the late Idris Hamid observed that God is largely represented in Caribbean worship and hymns as "a foreigner, a kind of White expatriate who is not God" of our own history, but an outsider, standing over and against Caribbean peoples.[26] In Australia, the legacy of missionary invaders remains strong on the liturgical forms of many Christian communities, and contemporary rhetoric of ecumenics, sometimes undergirded by liturgical means – the liturgical seasons, a common lectionary – are constant reminders of both origins and a centre of gravity elsewhere.[27]

As long as the perceptions and tastes of contemporary liturgical tradition remain largely Euro/Americo-centric, even though the centre of Christianity has been shifting for quite some time (and is also still largely within the male able-bodied and heterosexual domain), then postcolonial (as feminist and womanist scrutiny) ought to become and remain significant optics to help us rethink Christian worship and liturgy and reclaim the "theological surplus" that spins alternatives to empires.[28] A significant contribution of postcolonial theory and criticism, which we wish to draw on, is the way it has been able to "put issues relating to colonialism and imperialism at the centre of critical and intellectual enquiry" and to an extent enabled the interrogation and reconstruction of various subject areas within the disciplines of humanities and social sciences.[29]

The notion "postcolonial" is contentious in terms of the multiplicity of ways it is used.[30] It is a term, position or theory borrowed from literary studies and other disciplines as it offers some exciting possibilities for God-talk and religious discourse.[31] Postcolonialism, it has been noted, is not about the demise of colonialism as "post" as it embodies both "after" and "beyond." It is more about a critical stance, oppositional tactic or subversive reading strategy.

Postcolonialism is also an elusive term as it resists being classified, lacking fixity and exactness. This may be one reason why it appeals to us, as much of what we have inherited in our Christian traditions is the result of attempts to neatly parcel out notions of truth and doctrine. The postcolonial is characterized by open-ended discursive practices, border-crossings and interplay. Hence, in the context of biblical studies and theological discourse, R. S. Sugirtharah asserts that "postcolonial" shelters a range of distinct but related meanings. He writes:

> First, in a historical sense, it encapsulates the social, political and cultural conditions of the current world order, bringing to the fore the cultural, political and economic facts of colonialism, and aiding the recognition of the ambiguities of decolonialization and the ongoing recolonialization. Secondly, as a critical discursive practice, postcolonial criticism has initiated arresting analyses of texts and societies. It provides openings for oppositional readings, uncovers suppressed voices and, more pertinently, has as its foremost concern victims and their plight. It has not only interrogated colonial domination but has also offered viable critical alternatives. Thirdly, the term applies to the political and ideological stance of an interpreter who is engaged in anti-colonial and anti-globalizing theory and praxis. Applied to biblical studies, it seeks to uncover colonial designs in both biblical texts and their interpretation, and endeavours to read the text from such postcolonial concerns as identity, hybridity and diaspora. Unlike the current biblical scholarship produced, invigorated and contained by virtuous aspects of the Enlightenment and modernity, postcolonialism concentrates on the vicious aspects of modernity – colonialism and how its legacy influenced and informed the promotion of the Bible and the development of biblical interpretation.[32]

Themes such as hybrid, interstitial, intercultural, in-between, and counter-hegemonic, among others, will have bearing on the conversation we wish to encourage. Take the theme of hybridity, as one example in point. Kwok, drawing on the insights of Homi Bhabha,[33] writes:

> Cultural hybridity challenges the myths of purity of cultural lineage, homogeneity of identity, and monolithic understandings of national cultures. Hybridity in postcolonial discourse demystifies the power of representation, for it can function as camouflage, contest, or a space in-between so that denied knowledges can be articulated and recognized.[34]

Because a postcolonial theory and optics are committed to engage with cultural and textual articulations in the context of colonialism and neo-colonialism, it offers exciting possibilities to interrogate Christian worship, liturgical texts, symbols and hymnody – all central to the Christian faith – and their intertwined relationship with imperialism. Postcolonialism is primarily concerned with detecting, questioning, challenging and exposing how the dominated are represented by the dominant, the link between power and knowledge and the locating of ideologies in plots and characterization in texts and their interpretations.

What, for instance, in the arriving at and solidifying of early liturgical texts, happened to the marginal and dissenting voices? Why were some of these voices represented by the early church as heretical? What is the link between the deposit of faith, our liturgical texts/traditions, empire, the missionary enterprise, mission and theology? As Sugirtharajah poignantly observes, "Colonial discourse is staunchly wedded to unvarying and exclusive truth and tolerates no dissent or debate."[35] Postcolonial theory and optic is interested in the theologians' or hermeneutists' version of their reality and how that reality gets re-inscribed in interpretations including worship, liturgies and hymnody. Hence, postcolonial theory, as Kwok notes,

> offers an invaluable vantage point on theology, because it interrogates how religious and cultural productions are enmeshed in the economic and political domination of colonialism and empire building.[36]

In this process of interrogation the complex relationship between power and knowledge, centre and margin, the construction and representation of the marginalized, in the intertwining of global histories (centre and periphery) are highlighted. In the process, "clues for developing critical theological hermeneutics"[37] are explored and "the myth of cultural purity and colonialist disavowal"[38] are laid bare. For our purpose we wish to note two major foci of postcolonial studies that will be at the heart of this project. The first is the tactic of analysing the colonizers' strategies at constructing images of the colonized. The other focus is to understand how the colonized developed their own strategies for survival and self-representation.

The postcolonial optic affirms "a new mode of imagining, a new cultural logic, posited over against the Eurocentric monologic and the colonial manner of thinking and visioning reality."[39] The insights of postcolonial biblical/theological scholars who have employed this "tactic" or "stance" provide a framework for a critical scrutiny of liturgical discourse and texts necessary in the struggle for liberation. According to Christopher Duraisingh, the postcolonial imagination rejects the colonial tendency to "bifurcate reality and organize everyday life and discourse in terms of binaries" and to represent "identities as unified and fixed" rather than giving agency to their multiple, historical location and fluid nature.[40] Further, while the colonial imagination stifles diversity and difference with notions of unity, uniformity and sameness, "the postcolonial approach to reality is multicultural, reciprocal and dialogical" or *"multivoiced, dialogical and polycentric."*[41]

These insights provide us with a dynamic frame of reference to scrutinize liturgical texts for imperial and colonial influences, to engage, through the postcolonial optic, in a reconstructive reading of these texts and the liturgical discourse and to interrogate the "centre" from which these discourses are happening. In the process, questions such as the following become pertinent: Do the discourse, texts, symbols and imageries perpetuate bondage and notions of empire? How do they represent Black peoples, ethnic minorities, the Other, gender and sexuality? What do the symbols, the language and the shape of our liturgical/worship spaces, communicate *vis à vis* the agenda of empire/colonialism and the politics of location? What do they communicate in terms of inclusivity of recent migrants who have to re-negotiate sacred spaces?[42]

In our interest in the postcolonial optic we are also mindful of the danger of this tool becoming "bogged down" with its historical framework. As Sugirtharajah, the doyen of postcolonial biblical studies, observes: "[t]he interpreter has not only a discursive function but also an interventionist one which is ethically and ideologically committed." His words about "creative and productive future of postcolonial biblical criticism" and the need "to re-invent itself and enlarge its scope" is a timely reminder for our purposes as well. For our employment of the postcolonial optic to interrogate Christian worship, while it is geared at exposing "the power–knowledge axis" its double function is also to "move beyond abstract theorization and get involved in the day-to-day messy activities which affect people's lives."[43]

A Critical Overview of Liturgical Literature

Liturgical studies is a vibrant discipline, and the considerable range of concerns it embraces are suggested in Dwight Vogel's reader, *Primary Sources in Liturgical Theology*,[44] which purports to be the kind of textbook that might be used at graduate level as a comprehensive introduction to liturgical theology. It covers several broad areas, including methodology in liturgical theology, the relation of liturgy and theology, liturgy and living, and issues concerning language, word, and diversity. Over twenty-five extracts introduce the major contributions of (mainly) contemporary scholars, including among many others Gordon Lathrop, Gail Ramshaw and Don Saliers, whom Stephen mentioned earlier in this chapter as being key figures in his own engagement with and enthusiasm for the discipline. Vogel's collection is ecumenical, including several Roman Catholic, Lutheran, Methodist, and Reformed perspectives, with less from Orthodox and Pentecostal and radical-Reformation sources, and interestingly there is only one reading from an Anglican, Evelyn Underhill – so that, in fact, no living Anglicans are represented.

Primary Sources in Liturgical Theology includes material from both women and men, and a small percentage of material from "persons of colour." It is, however, heavily weighted to North American contributions to the discipline, not least because it draws upon primary sources and brief commentary from leading figures in the North American Academy of Liturgy, which, with *Societas Liturgica*, is one of the key communities that supports persons engaged in liturgical work both in the North American context and beyond. As its title suggests, it also self-consciously focuses on contributions to liturgical *theology*, and while by no means disregarding liturgical history, necessarily pushes historical considerations somewhat to one side in order to focus on its principally theological concerns. Hence, the preface of Vogel's book notes that the likes of Paul Bradshaw, Josef Jungmann and James White – persons known primarily for their work on the history of the liturgy – are not included. In this feature, the collection betrays the fact that liturgical theology is an approach to the broader area of liturgical study that is not the only possible one, and indeed, that an emphasis on liturgical theology may be more common in the USA and Canada than elsewhere. In the UK, by contrast, the study of Christian worship tends to have been fostered around historical trajectories, with Paul Bradshaw, himself an English Anglican, exemplifying this approach in the like of his *Search for the Origins of Christian Worship*,[45] which is undoubtedly one of the key late-twentieth-century texts in liturgical studies. The historical bent of his explorations is conveyed in the "origins" of the title, and is echoed in other work, such as his *Eucharistic Origins*.[46]

The denominational weighting of Vogel's book also in large part reflects the traditions which participate in the World Council of Churches. Liturgical renewal has long been allied to ecumenism.[47] The WCC has largely been constituted by old-line Protestant churches – albeit with Roman Catholic "observation" – although it is now making concerted efforts to embrace traditions that had hitherto not been central to its make-up, namely the Orthodox, Pentecostal and the successors of the radical Reformation.[48] Of course, within the latter two of these three broad groupings, many non-European Christian communities are situated, and, as with a number of old-line church-styles, movements such as Pentecostalism with origins in the northern hemisphere are demonstrably part of a shift of force to the so-called "global south."

Christian Worship: A Postcolonial Scrutiny

We hope that our dialogical and contrapuntal conversation with each other and various interlocutors will underscore the inter-disciplinary, conversational/dialogical, and critical nature of this engagement. Further, our collaborative approach emphasizes our commitment to dialogue across disciplines and modelling contra-puntal engagement as an academic habit. Moreover, working across distances by geography, time, space and national traditions alongside the fact that we are both "aliens" or "diasporans" will highlight not only differences in our orientations and criticality but will also help us scrutinize our own designed cultural assumptions. We trust that what is brought together here embraces a more expansive view that would have been limited by an individual point of view.

What is offered here, then, is "fragments" of a discourse that underscore the tentativeness of what we see as an ongoing, inter-disciplinary and intercultural conversation. Here we take heart and are encouraged with the insight of Walter Brueggemann that can very well apply to how we perceive the nature of the undertaking. He writes:

> It is not, in my judgment the work of the Church (or of the preacher) to construct a full alternative word, for that would be to act pre-emptively and imperialistically as all those old construals and impositions. Rather, the task is to *fund* – to provide the pieces, materials and resources out of which a new world can be imagined. Our responsibility, then, is not a grand scheme or a coherent system, but the voicing of a lot of little pieces out of which people can put life together in *fresh configurations*.[49]

It is our wish that this volume will offer insights to stir and fund the imagination that will open up ways to decolonize our mental moulds and break what "seems to be endless cycles of self-preferentiality"[50] which we are locked, knowingly or unknowingly, by imperial habits. We further hope that our conversation will create vistas that will generate new ways of perceiving through the much needed decolo-nization of worship and liturgy and their concomitant texts.

Part Two

The Mixed Media of Liturgy

2 Liturgical Texts and Symbolic Contexts

Introducing the Conversation

R. S. Sugirtharajah's critique of systematic theology can very well apply to liturgical studies and Christian worship.[1] Sugirtharajah, one of the key voices on postcolonial biblical hermeneutics, writes:

> ...what is striking about systematic theology is the reluctance of its practitioners to address the relation between European colonialism and the field. There has been a marked hesitancy to critically evaluate the impact of the empire among systematic theologians, both during and after the European expansion. Theologians in the West cannot excuse themselves by suggesting that the empire had little impact "at home." New studies in literature, visual culture, geography and history in the last decade have demonstrated the numerous ways in which the empire was central to English domestic life and popular consciousness.[2]

Although rigorous postcolonial perspectives are now developing in the areas of hermeneutics, biblical studies, feminist theology,[3] and to a lesser degree systematic theology[4] to scrutinize imperial and cultural texts for their support of the colonial agenda, the study of Christian worship, as we have noted, is as yet to be critically scrutinized through the optic of a sustained and developed postcolonial critique.

The failure of liturgical studies to appropriate the insights of postcolonial criticism, hermeneutics and theology is startlingly evident, in that although it includes a full-length article on "inculturation" by Anscar Chupungco there is still a marked absence of an entry on "postcolonialism" in the recently revised *New SCM Dictionary of Liturgy and Worship*.[5] Moreover, the recent *SCM Dictionary of Third World Theologies* includes a brief article by Margaret Shanthi on "worship/rituals" which consists, in the main part, of discussion of issues relating to inculturation.[6]

Beyond Inculturation

In our view, a postcolonial perspective on Christian worship, liturgical studies, hymnody, among other areas, will clearly want to build on the notion and practice of inculturation. However, a postcolonial reading will want to include more than that. Significantly, it will also be critical of and question the very notion of inculturation, how it is employed and whether it is another form of hegemonic control, empire building and colonization. For, as Musa Dube notes, imperializing texts assumes "many forms" and can come from the pen of "the colonized who either collaborate with the dominant forces or yearn for the same power."[7] How such an ensuing and necessary conversation will develop may not seem clear at the moment given the paucity in this area.[8] What is clear in our minds, however, is the need to do so and the insights that can be gleaned from the ongoing conversations on the influence of postcolonial studies in the areas of biblical studies, hermeneutics and, more recently, theology.

With regard to the observation that postcolonial studies as employed in the areas noted above are yet to penetrate the domain of Christian worship and liturgical studies, a likely reason may be located in the fact that *liturgical* discussions on inculturation tend to take as their cue the Second Vatican Council's liturgy document *Sacrosanctum Concilium*. Specifically, paragraphs 37–40 underscore the concern with "legitimate variations and adaptations" of the Roman rite to "different groups, regions and peoples, especially in mission countries." Naturally, the agenda of inculturation within this framework will not concern itself with notions of empire, colonialism, vested political interests and the relationship of these to the teachings of the Roman Church (and other Churches), especially as these are conveyed in the symbols, language and imageries of the Church and embodied in the liturgical texts.[9]

In liturgical studies, inculturation has generated a significant amount of discussion, most obviously associated with the name of Oscar Chupungco, the author of the article in the *New SCM Dictionary of Liturgy and Worship*.[10] He summarizes his own view as being that "liturgical pluralism is an incarnational imperative, rather than a concession of Vatican II."[11] Examples of liturgical inculturation or incarnation include the possible use of texts – such as scripture from other faith-traditions proclaimed in the context of Christian worship – as well as gesture, posture, ceremony and song from non-centralized sources; that is, in the Roman Catholic context, not from European directives.

This is an interesting insight by Chupungco that a postcolonial reading will want to question and be in conversation with. For instance, what is the relationship between inculturation and appropriation of the cultural practices of marginalized groups into the practices of a dominant group? Myke Johnsont, writing in a different context (that of the cultural appropriation of Native Americans symbols and ceremonies), can help elucidate this point. Johnsont writes:

> Cultural appropriation is a form of racism. Cultural appropriation is a weapon in the process of colonization. Cultural appropriation is when a dominating [group] or colonizing people take over the cultural and religious ceremonies and articles of a people experiencing domination or colonization. When Euro-Americans take Native American symbols and ceremonies and use them for our own purposes, we are participating in the process of colonization and the destruction of Native culture.[12]

While we do not subscribe to the notion of a "pure" culture, but rather the complex and dialogical nature of cultures in relationship to and encounter with each other, we are sympathetic to Johnsont's view for the fact that it raises some important questions from a postcolonial perspective. These include the end of inculturation, the implied and overt view that sees the native peoples' cultural practices as childish, superstitious and under-developed, and the relationship between cultural appropriation, the assertion of a dominant group as the harbinger of a civilized/enlightened/rational ethos and the marginalization and the eventual disappearance of native symbolisms. Perhaps a connection with vernacular hermeneutics may further sharpen the critical nature of the questions raised here. While culture becomes an important location for the process of inculturation, one can ask, borrowing from Sugirtharajah: how much of inculturation is about "disturb[ing] and dislodge[ing] the reigning imported themes"?[13] How can we ensure that the cultural and ideological assumptions are not re-positioned or re-inserted in the acculturation or translation process?[14] An honest answer to these questions will reveal why liturgical studies are yet to be viewed through the postcolonial optic. This is more than urgent given the fact of western Christianity's link to the colonial agenda.[15]

Moreover, it should be noted that since the implementation of the provisions for adaptation at Vatican II, the Roman Catholic authorities have become increasingly reserved about the implications of such provision, fearing fracture of the "unity" of expression of Catholic faith.[16] The official caution with the so-called "Zaire Mass" is well-documented elsewhere and shows how the development of much of what might have been achieved in the initial vision of *Sacrosanctum Concilium* has in fact been stalled. In any case, it might well be argued that *Sacrosanctum Concilium* was in the first place over-prescriptive in its proviso that any such adaptations must "harmonize with" the "true and authentic spirit" of rites imported/imposed from elsewhere, which reveals the essentially ancillary nature of whatever may come to be incorporated into localized forms of Christian worship.

So, although inculturation is of undoubted importance to liturgical studies and integral to the postcolonial discourse, it stops short of the kinds of "reconfigurations" emerging in a postcolonial approach to the other disciplines within the theological enterprise.

The Postcolonial Optic

The insights of postcolonial biblical/theological scholars such as Sugirtharajah, Musa Dube, Fernando Segovia and Kwok Pui-lan (among others) do provide a framework for a critical scrutiny of liturgical discourse and texts necessary in the struggle for liberation. Their insights provide us with a dynamic frame of reference to scrutinize liturgical texts for their imperial and colonial influences, to engage, through the postcolonial optic, in a reconstructive reading of these texts and the liturgical discourse and to interrogate the "centre" from which these discourses are happening. In the process, questions such as the following become pertinent: Do the discourse, texts, symbols and imageries perpetuate bondage and notions of empire? How do they represent Black peoples, ethnic minorities, the Other, gender and sexuality? What do the symbols, the language and the shape of our liturgical/worship spaces communicate *vis à vis* the agenda of empire/colonialism and the politics of location? What do they communicate in terms of inclusivity of recent migrants who have to re-negotiate sacred spaces?[17]

In commencing a necessary conversation between the emerging discipline of postcolonial theology and liturgical studies, this chapter proposes to use some questions raised by a particular act of worship in which we both shared as a modest way of opening up debate about the implications of postcolonial awareness. Some of these insights we will then pursue in the succeeding chapters.

A Recurring Problem

An example of the need for a postcolonial critique forcefully came to our attention recently in an ecumenical service for the Women's World Day of Prayer. This day of prayer is an internationally and trans-denominationally significant event that takes place each year. For the day of prayer (March 4, 2005), materials promoted for international use were based on resources compiled by "Christian Women of Poland." The theme they adopted was "Let our Light Shine." Unsurprisingly, given this theme, the service employed abundant use of the imagery of "light," as in the following example:

> We pray together:
> **that the light of God's word may speak in us;**
> **that the light of God's Spirit may enliven us;**
> **that the fervour of God's love may inspire us.**
> God is brightening our darkness,
> so that we may, as reflections of God's light,
> be light for those who still remain in darkness.

The prayer-texts used in the Polish women's service, as well as scripture readings and songs, all amplified the same "kinds" of imagery. Hence, in Ephesians 5:8-11, we read: "you were once in darkness, but now you are light in the Lord." We sang, "God, whose almighty word / chaos and darkness heard"; "Longing for light / we wait in darkness"; "Lord, the light of your love is shining." The symbolic focus and liturgical action centred on lighted candles – first of all candles placed on the holy table, then being ritually lit from person to person throughout the assembly.

However, each of these aspects of the service – in its play and use of light and darkness – is problematic if, as our colleague Mukti Barton contends, "racism is perpetuated when the colour Black is used in negative, and White in positive, ways," and these associations arise from European interpretations of the Bible's use of light and darkness imagery.[18]

Part of Barton's argument is that in some languages – including her own Bengali – Blackness and darkness are quite distinct, although in English, the overlapping of the two terms are much more ambiguous, at times "synonymous."[19] Consequently, European interpretations of the Bible – itself "from the East" – and its imagery may muddle "originally biblical" and "purely European" meanings, leading to both confusion and harm. The extent and complexity of this "muddling" has been disclosed in Gay L. Byron's scholarly work *Symbolic Blackness and Ethnic Difference in Early Christian Literature*. Here, she highlights the fact of ethno-political rhetoric in the discourses of ancient Christian writers (some influential voices in early liturgical documents) and their employment of the Black One/Blackness/Ethiopian/Darkness as tropes of the spiritual and political threats that challenged the en*light*ened, spiritual, civilized and monochrome world of the dominant culture. Hence, "[a]mong patristic writers, darkness became a major theme for discussing the presence of sin. Light came to the Gentiles once they turned from their life of sin."[20] Both Barton and Byron build on Robert Hood's *Begrimed and Black: Christian Traditions on Black and Blackness* whose critical examination of various ancient sources highlights the ideological bias against Blacks/Blackness in these Christian sources and the consequent negative representations of the "Other." Thus,

> Blackness in early Christian thought overwhelmingly conveyed social values and a moral rank subordinate to Whiteness, an attitude that became a cornerstone of Western cultural views reinforced by the slave trade, economics, Egyptology, physical and social sciences, and later Christendom.[21]

This bias and prejudice is not an issue of bygone generations. Recently in France, a White French woman claimed an ethnic "Other" attacked her and her infant on a train. She then proceeded to give a vivid description of her phantom and evil "Arab"-looking attacker. There was a national outcry at this bestial behaviour to a mother and her small child. It was later disclosed that she had lied about the whole incident. It would not be difficult to find similar incidents in the UK and USA. The question is not why people would go to such an extent to lie and provide such vivid description, but why would the major part of the population believe it. Negative signification of "Other"/"Blacks" and its influence on us is a real and present issue. For the language of signifying is not value free; it is created by the group with power to "lock down" the signified in their place: twenty sub-human rungs below the signifier.[22]

Our experience of the above cited service raises many interesting points of departure for a postcolonial critique of Christian worship as it may be celebrated in the West, and suggests some hard and critical questions about how such a range of imagery might be appropriated in non-western contexts. The scriptures, hymnody, gestures and symbols employed in the service each require critical attention, for each of these aspects of the liturgical environment and dynamic might be employed in ways that most unhelpfully amplify one trajectory of imagery without giving room to complementary or conflicting strands of the liturgical tradition and its sources, not least scripture (the latter of which Barton subjects to extensive evaluation in the article to which we have referred).

The Women's World Day of Prayer also raises difficult questions for a postcolonial critique of western liturgical texts. Poland, the source of the 2005 service, does not have the obvious "colonizing" history of other European nations, and in fact in the twentieth century underwent marked national suffering at the hands of invading nations, as seen in the way in which its "liberation" was a major focus of attention during mourning for Pope John Paul II. This resists any over-simple alliance of this "second-world" nation with "first-world" western nations as well as hinting at some persistent ambiguities in the perpetuation of Catholic tradition under a Pope in large part responsible for both the redefinition of a national identity and the enveloping reserve of contemporary Catholic authorities concerning the localization of liturgical celebration. Moreover, while Poland may not have a "colonizing" history, it has received and has subscribed to Catholicism with a history that went hand in glove with the European colonial expansionist agenda. As Musa Dube reminds us (cited earlier), imperializing texts come in various disguises, including the pen of the colonized in collaboration with the dominant group mimicking the same power,[23] underscoring the complex nature of the issue before us.

Revising Language and Texts

No doubt most of us are afraid of the darkness – especially if you are a child and cannot see in the dark. The problematic, however, is what the White imagination has done in transferring this terror of darkness to whole ethnicities. Be it a White writer, painter, dramatist, theologian, or news reporter, an evil, ugly or monstrous character would more than likely to be represented as black/dark.

One of the key features of the colonial agenda is control over language. Hence, both Dube and Sugirtharajah, *inter alia*, in the context of biblical studies and hermeneutics, are closely scrutinizing the various forms of representations in the texts and the different ways that these are implicated in the imperial agenda and consequent oppression of the "subaltern." Representations are never exact or value free. As Edward Said has demonstrated in *Orientalism*, representations as constructed images are not harmless likenesses. They convey messages that influence the ways the Orient and its natives are perceived. They need to be interrogated for their ideological content.[24] Frantz Fanon has argued that colonization by a language impacts significantly upon one's consciousness. The fact of speaking the "oppressors'" language, be it French or English, would necessarily mean, for the colonized, an acceptance of the collective consciousness of those nations and their identification of "Blackness" or "darkness" with evil and sin. Hence, the Black person wears a White mask and becomes some imaginary universal subject working towards building that beloved community minus his or her personal appearance.[25] This raises a serious question for the process of inculturation and the role of our liturgical texts in the process of internalizing a consciousness that accepts as normal a disjuncture between a Black person's (or a minority ethnic person's) consciousness and his or her body and physical features. Through such internalization, liturgy and worship becomes an oppressive act – whatever/whomsoever the agency.

Given that the category of "White" depends for its functioning on a negation of "Black," and cognizant of the ways in which Eurocentric interpretation of "light" and "darkness" imageries might strengthen negative associations of Blackness, the Women's World Day of Prayer service invites the question of how it is desirable and necessary to develop radical alternative language. In fact, Fanon would contend that an entirely new world and new mindset must be ushered in – a total revolution is needed.[26] Whatever one's take on Fanon's challenge, the relevant point for us is the demanding nature and urgent need for new and liberating language and metaphors. To critically confront and engage our beliefs, values, prejudices and assumptions in order to make sense or discern how they evolved and have become a natural part of one's life is very demanding. And the reality is: for the dominant to enter the space of the subjugated and learn how to exist in that space is an enormous and costly challenge.

As a positive suggestion, perhaps some of the difficulties we noted in the *Women's World Day of Prayer* could be minimized by replacing the language of light with that of "radiance" or "brightness." The idea of divine brightness was in fact expressed in the Women's World Day of Prayer Service we attended, but only in close connection with the language of light, and so it suffered from associated negative connotations. However, detached from the language of light, "bright" and "radiant" imply no particular colour, avoiding dehumanizing associations. Likewise, the language of darkness can be replaced by the more shifting notion of "shadows." Again, this implies no particular colour. Prayers such as those found in the Women's World Day of Prayer service could then be re-worded to avoid language that is potentially offensive, reinforces stereotypes, systems of inequality and subordination and prejudices and is harmful in its use.

However, it should be noted that were such rewording to be worked consistently through current liturgical provisions, the task would be enormous because the worship resources of many European churches are insensitively unconscientized to the difficulties of light and darkness imagery – not to mention those that are suffused with notions of empire. As just one example, the Church of England's *Common Worship* resource for daily prayer makes much use of the imagery, indeed accentuating it throughout the Christmas cycle of seasons from Advent through to Candlemas. Furthermore, the ancient office of the *Lucernarium* – lamp-lighting – has also been revived in many of the current provisions across the Christian traditions, requiring caution about the language of light in that context also, which is one for which a plethora of new prayers have recently been written.

One liturgical theologian who has given some thought to at least some of the problems associated with the extensive use of the language of light in the liturgy is Gail Ramshaw, whose work on liturgical language has expressed the dual aims of "keeping it metaphoric" and "making it inclusive." We note that Ramshaw's critique does not derive directly from the postcolonial optic. Rather, her main motivations are (White) feminist: for instance, her particular agenda comes to the fore in her concluding comments on talk of the kingdom, as she suggests that "images of Christ will give us quite enough male imagery: we can no longer defend its use for God."[27] In her work *Liturgical Language*, she tackles four images central to Christian liturgy: "the kingdom of God," "the body of Christ," "Egypt" and "blindness."

The second, "the body of Christ," Ramshaw regards as unproblematic as this is "much more inclusive than the image of 'the family of God,' and not as andocentric" for starters.[28] This may be so, but questions that the postcolonial agency will want to pursue include: what is the relationship of that body which was strung up on the tree of a cross with the whipping and hanging of Black slaves hung to a tree and the continuing "incarceration" of Black humanity? How have we represented and how do we continue to represent that body in our texts and visually? What is that disfigured body – not a perfect one – saying to a theology and liturgy shaped in the framework of the "perfect" and "sinless" body? In a religiously plural context, what kind of polemics and (ethno)rhetoric will shape our discourse on the "body of Christ" imagery as inclusive? A cursory glance at the theology in the era of missions and colonial expansion will reveal how the body of the natives has been represented as Black, dirty, ugly, sinful, uncivilized, the embodiment of the heats of carnal desire and had been used negatively in the polemics of taking the message to the gentiles. In the Euro-centric collective consciousness, "the Body of Christ" may be more problematic than we assume it to be.

In the absence of developed postcolonial critiques of liturgy, however, a first stage towards galvanizing of such critiques may be to learn from associated or related critical perspectives. Hence, we want to affirm that Ramshaw's contributions are significant – especially her discourse on the flawed nature of the other three images, the alternative metaphors she suggests in order to rescue some of the notions, and the implications of these in the light of the postcolonial discourse. The first of Ramshaw's chosen foci – "the kingdom of God" – has much of relevance to offer in terms of its link to the agenda of colonial domination; her third chosen focus – "Egypt" – raises questions about the representation of the "Other"; and her fourth chosen focus – "blindness" – underscores the problematic with the language of light. Clues as to how language can be reformed for the better might be gleaned from all of her examples. Some of her suggested alternative metaphors, however, highlight the need for a critical conversation via the postcolonial optic.

According to Ramshaw, the trouble with "the kingdom" centres on what she calls in another place "the myth of the crown."[29] In short, "God is not a male deity rewarding a superhuman warrior with absolute authority over a dependent population."[30]

Language that suggests otherwise is in her judgement prey to both totalitarianism and infantilism. By way of constructive alternatives, she suggests that the words "sovereign" and "monarch" are possible non-gendered alternatives to language of kingship; and that "reign," "dominion" and "commonwealth" might retranslate "kingdom."[31] In her work to provide the churches with an inclusive-language version of the lectionary, Ramshaw tends to opt for the image of the "dominion of God."[32] While the postcolonial critic will have little difficulty in juxtaposing God's dominion (or for that matter commonweal or community) against that of colonial (old and new) hegemony, these alternatives are still problematic. These may be non-gendered, but they still smack of the language of "empire," power and "domination" – even though it is God's. The fundamental issue from a postcolonial reading is what actually remains unquestioned: the underlying assumption of superiority or privilege that is assumed by one group or nation under the guise of working on behalf of the reign of this monarch. Hence, God, the monarch, calls a chosen nation(s) out to usher in God's dominion, to lord it over backward and uncivilized natives. A scrutiny of the speeches of the president of God's only nation on earth just before and after the Iraq war reinforces how real and present is this danger. The point is that such alternatives can just as well provide another garb for imperial self-justification. "Our theological ventures," reminds Marion Grau, "can represent God, though they are always in danger of misrepresenting God."[33]

The image of "Egypt" comes into focus in liturgical tradition in association with Triduum celebrations, with the paschal mystery related to exodus, and in that context Egypt is associated with the "perennial powers of evil and death," a shorthand to "denote the reality of evil."[34] Said's work in *Orientalism* is helpful here. From a postcolonial perspective Said shows how Orientalism is "a western style for dominating restructuring, and having authority over the Orient."[35] Hence, the Orient is conceptualized and represented in terms of difference, backwardness, strangeness, feminine penetrability, and lack of civilization. The overarching agenda of Orientalism, as Said contends, is a self-justification of western hegemony over the "Egypts" of this world. As a result of which, textual representations, including liturgical texts as constructed images, need to be interrogated to denude their ideological content. As Ramshaw points out, ancient documentation from non-Hebrew sources contain no memories of Pharaoh enslaving their neighbours into forced labour. At the very least, as part of our liturgical language, "Egypt" requires "careful catechesis."[36]

The language of blindness is also problematic not only because of its vulnerability to association with the championing of light and disparagement of darkness in relation to skin pigmentation, but also because of its liability to prove offensive for other reasons to those who are visually impaired. It is in fact the latter of these circumstances upon which Ramshaw principally comments, and it is one that our colleague John Hull has explored at length in his book *In the Beginning There was Darkness*.[37] For her part, Ramshaw asserts that

> obviously offensive renderings must be discarded... The condition [of blindness] must never become the entire person... Homilies and

catechesis must never use the image to suggest stupidity. Most important, inspired by the dialogue in John 9, Christians ought never to construe disabilities as examples of punishment.[38]

While this is commendable it does not extend to the problematic language of light and darkness and its potential to dehumanize some persons in terms of Barton's and Byron's concerns. Ramshaw may be cognizant of this for she counsels that "since no symbolic imagery works perfectly for all, it is good that a great variety of images is available."[39] At the very least, this commends the kind of expansiveness that is not at present apparent in most of the ways that the language of light and darkness is employed in western liturgies.

Other examples include John Bell's hymn "Thank You for the Night" which is a rare instance of the language of darkness being employed positively in the setting of liturgy. It is written with vespers especially in mind and it allows for some of the variety Ramshaw commends. The hymn also underscores the enormous challenge before us as is evident from stanza four where Bell's mind, unconsciously and because of years of conditioning, somersaults back into the default mode. Why should the opening lines of that stanza not read: "Thank you for the word, which neither darkness nor light can contain"? The text reads:

> Thank you for the night / the sign that day is done / that life is meant to rest and sleep to come. / Thank you for the quiet / as silence scatters sound, / while God, in both, / is waiting to be found. / Thank you for the dark / to complement the light, / as insight, open-eyed, / replaces sight. / Thank you for the word, / which darkness can't contain, / that life, laid down, / is raised to life again. / Thank you for the night, / a measure of your care. / In darkness, as in light, / you, Lord, are there.[40]

Interestingly, another intriguing potential way forward in continued use of light and darkness imagery – albeit best contained within a more expansive repertoire – emerges in the recent liturgical provisions for the Anglican Church of Kenya. *Our Modern Services* is replete with imagery of light and darkness, and it must be said that it is not always possible to imagine how it could escape the kind of critique to which Barton and Byron subject appropriation of such imagery from scriptural sources. However, in commentary about how the language of "light" is used in the book, it is at least sometimes configured above all with "weight" as this contributes to the meaning of "glory," rather than with "darkness" as a symbol of blindness, lostness or sin. For example, the confession used in morning and evening prayer reads in part:

> **We have done wrong and neglected to do right;**
> **our sins weigh heavily on our hearts;**
> **Lord, have mercy, count them not against us.**
> **Grant us the joy of forgiveness**
> **and lighten our hearts with the glory of Christ,**
> **who died and rose again for us.**[41]

While the deliberate alliance of lightness and heaviness may indeed be missed by most people, the Kenyan confession is perhaps a good example of the potential for reconfiguration of familiar imagery drawing on alternative but yet deeply embedded scriptural allusions. It might well, then, fruitfully be subject to the careful catechesis that Ramshaw commends in relation to the church's liturgical language.

The Issue of Representation: Symbolism and the Symbolic

In *Beyond Colonial Anglicanism*, Glauco S. de Lima writes in the preface:

> In our Anglican churches, the signs and the power of colonial symbols may be seen not only in the liturgical order. The Hebrew and Greek sources of our liturgy come to us already filtered through British culture and in the Book of Common Prayer, a wonderful Western and Christian inspiration, itself an example of a contextual theological process. Beyond the very order and the linguistic sources of our worship, even our clothing bears a witness to a colonial origin. In the vestments and trimmings of the clergy, for example, on the bishop's surplice, the sleeves finish up at the cuffs in the same way as those of the nobleman in the British court.[42]

As we have emphasized, our liturgical texts and symbols are laced with ideological and cultural presuppositions of one dominant group. We now turn our focus to symbols and symbolic representations.

The works of Said, Spivak, Sugirtharajah and Musa Dube *et al.* reveal that symbols are constructed images/representations. These are never value free. They are intended to communicate a message and shape a view or opinion. They have a semiotic meaning – where something "stands for" something else. Worship texts and liturgical symbols/gestures are not mere pointers and ends in themselves. What they are pointing to and the meanings they convey are crucial. In other words, what are the cultural, religious, political and ideological interests and contexts from which these symbols and representations emerge?[43] Representations or the symbols/images cultivated and nurtured in the "mind" have enormous implications for "flesh and blood" people in real contexts. The early calls of Bob Marley, Marcus Garvey and Frantz Fanon (to a lesser extent) for emancipation from "mental slavery" underscore the nature of the challenge and its radical demands.

As noted, the common action of lamp-lighting was involved in the Women's World Day of Prayer service we attended. There is no reason to complain about this in itself, so long as it can be detached from negative associations of colour. However, Inderjit Bhogal's presence with us on the particular occasion of the Polish women's liturgy reminded us of the importance of attending to the full range of symbolic dimensions of liturgy. Bhogal is known for his critique of the *Methodist Worship Book*'s rubric requiring that "a white cloth" covers the remains of eucharistized elements of holy communion.[44] This mandate itself echoes that of the Church of England's *Book of Common Prayer* (1662) which instructs that

> when all have communicated, the Minister shall return to the Lord's Table, and reverently place upon it what remaineth of the consecrated Elements, covering the same with a fair linen cloth,[45]

a practice also transmitted to subsequent Anglican liturgical practice. Of course, as with the scriptural words explored by Barton, "fair" need not mean "White,"[46] although the possibility of alternatives is crushed by the *Methodist Worship Book*.

Our unease with this is that close association of "fairness" or particularly "Whiteness" and sacramentality generates a dismally unhelpful visual theology. Apart from whatever care is taken over what words are chosen at particular parts of the liturgy, or about scriptural translation, indefensible symbolic alliances may be set up between colour and holiness in the visual dimensions of sacramental celebration. Why, for instance, are wafers always white? At the very least, Barton's reminders about the ambiguity of biblical references to Whiteness – diseased skin, as in Exod. 4:6, Num. 12:10 and 2 Kgs 5:27, and the anti-christic white horse of Rev. 6:2, for instance – are important things to recall in contest to any naïve resonance of colour in the liturgy. The question then is why aren't multi-coloured cloths at the communion table[47] symbolic of the rainbow of divine promise.

A postcolonial perspective will find some common cause with the feminist consciousness espoused by Gail Ramshaw and learn from feminists/womanists engaged in liturgy to look beyond the words to consider and construct a wealth of "gestures of resistance."[48] As Janet Walton elaborates:

> Horizontal gestures prevail in feminist liturgies; they suggest equality and interdependence; they affirm God known among us. Generally we do not look up to find God. We connect with each other to give and receive blessings. We pray with our eyes open and without bowing our heads. Not that we do not acknowledge God's authority, but we know God does not require bowing our heads and closing our eyes. Bowing our heads for a blessing, as Marjorie Proctor-Smith points out, is "a non-reciprocal action" related to experiences that remind us of a male domination. It signals an inferior social status that has not promoted women's well-being. Closing one's eyes is dangerous in an unjust society. Though we presume we are safe in our gatherings, we do not repeat actions that have historically limited, demeaned or hurt us.
>
> Kneeling poses problems, too. We recognize its value to remind us of reverence for God and one another, but when women kneel to receive Communion or a blessing from men, rather than promoting an experience of reverence, it can be a reminder of sexual violation or subservience. Since women are frequently victims of violence at the hands of men, we practice standing and sitting rather than kneeling. We want to remind ourselves every time we can that sexual violence is rooted in misplaced power, that is, when anyone presumes power over another. Feminist liturgies intend to provide occasions to practice gestures of resistance and expressions of shared power.[49]

Clearly, there is much in the above observations by Walton that the postcolonial critic will affirm and concur with. One of the implications of the foregoing is about self-representation and raises a number of questions. Who decides on symbols and representations? Is it the centre of authority, the dominant culture or the marginal voices? "Can the subaltern speak?" as Spivak asks in her seminal essay. Spivak contends that representation is a form of speech act implying a speaker and a listener. She observes that when the subaltern/colonized or person on the margins engages at self-representation, often outside "the lines laid down by the official institutional structures of representation,"[50] such representations are usually not recognized by the listener. Hence, Spivak's contention that representation in this context seems almost impossible. Spivak's observation is helpful in highlighting the complex nature of who speaks for whom and self-representation. Spivak's interjection about the nearly impossible task of self-representation does mean that we should not underestimate the task of challenging status quo representations and their ideological agenda in reinforcing systems of inequality and subordination.

Developing a postcolonial critique of the liturgy will mean combing the actions of the assembly with these and other gestures in mind and at the same time asking the critical questions. To dislodge dominant and oppressive modes of representing and imaging demands nothing less. It will mean cultivating and nurturing safe, fluid ecclesial spaces to enable such critical questions by the subaltern communities. This is more than using Nan bread, wearing colourful Ghanaian vestments, covering the table with multi-coloured cloth or striking a Tibetan gong during our worship. Our (new) metaphors and symbols would challenge any notion of wanting to neatly appropriate differences. They ought to elude the dominant or status quo proclivity to define and control.

Concluding Observations

A postcolonial scrutiny of liturgical/worship texts exposes the issues of the ideological and colonial agenda of western Christianity. It also problematizes, as we have demonstrated, the issues of language, imageries, symbols and representations in our liturgical/worship texts and symbols. Hence, a postcolonial perspective on the worship offered by Christian assemblies matters for all kinds of reasons. At a macro-level, the development and demise of liturgical inculturation illustrates at least the potential threat to centralized liturgical authorities of those whose cultural inheritance is not Euro-centric and may be variously hybrid. At the micro-level, we have tried to open up by a focus on just some of the problems knotted into just one service, and have suggested a comprehensive range of matters for consideration and contest, revision and reform. Most minimally, the development of informed and authentic postcolonial critiques of Christian worship is necessary in order to enact Margaret Shanthi's conclusion to her article "Worship/rituals" in the *SCM Dictionary of Third World Theologies*: "Worship that legitimizes classism, racism, casteism, and sexism is dehumanizing and alienating. True worship is that which liberates and calls people to wholeness."[51] And the point is not simply that "inclusivity" is important, but perhaps ultimately that

> A deepening sense of "being church" is … part of the unexpected side of the work of inclusion. The movement from adopting an "inclusive" attitude on the part of the leadership to the actual life of being a place of "belonging" is itself a *maturation*, both theological and moral. This … is part of what it means to be a *faithful people of God* in the world, to "grow up in every way" into Christ (Ephesians 4:15). Participating in the movement from inclusivity to the spirituality of belonging to one another is an image of the Christian life itself.[52]

The question still to be considered, however, is what such "maturation" in our journey of faith and faithfulness in God in Christ means. Will it mean merely being confined to bringing out the meaning of texts, or occasionally protecting them from "wayward" misreadings? Or would one implication be that when the moment dawns on us faith-fulness will require of us the courage to be "prepared to give up the very text themselves"?[53]

3 Embodying Theology in Song

Rule now on earth from realms above
Subdue the nations by thy love.
And all the earth, redeemed by thee,
Shall know a glorious liberty
(O Christ the Lord, O Christ the king:
R. T. Brooks 1918–85, in the *New English Hymnal*)

Introducing the Conversation

Within the Christian community, hymns, songs and music have a significant place. One can reasonably contend that Christian liturgy was born singing.[1] Hymns, however, are more than praise, prayer, poetry and liturgy. They also embody what we believe (doctrine and theology). This is because imperializing texts assume "many forms" and "shapes" and those from the pen of hymn writers are no exception.[2] In the last chapter we noted that hymnody, among other elements of our worship, requires critical attention. This chapter is an attempt to engage in a similar critical conversation but with a more intentional focus on our hymns and hymnals. As Charlotte Kroeker notes, church music "is in the service of the liturgy" and "at its best is a way to understand theology." In other words, both liturgy and theology matters and hymns may play a crucial role in both.[3]

In Chapter 2 we located the problematic by raising some questions that are also applicable to the conversation we intend in this present chapter. We will do well to remind ourselves of some of these questions: Do the discourse, texts, symbols and imageries (of the hymns) perpetuate bondage and notions of empire? How do they represent Black peoples, ethnic minorities, the Other, gender and sexuality? What do symbols and language communicate *vis à vis* the agenda of empire/colonialism and the politics of location? When is inculturation and the appropriation of other people's songs and music another form of exploitation or a new kind of colonialism? These framing questions ought to enable our critical scrutiny of hymns and hymnals of Christian communities.

A postcolonial gaze at hymns, hymnals and hymnody is both exciting and daunting. It is exciting because of the need to highlight the link between the European colonial agenda and the expansion of European Christianity and also because there is an urgent need for such a scrutiny. The daunting nature can be located in the demands of the undertaking given that such a gaze is yet to be developed and we are working into a hugely underdeveloped area within the inevitable limitations of a short chapter. Hence, our undertaking can only be considered tentative and as part of a longer process.

Employing the Postcolonial Gaze: Singing via a Different Optic

In Chapter 1, we have already introduced the postcolonial optic. Applied to the task before us – hymns, hymnals and the theology they espouse – the postcolonial optic allows us to undress the "colonial designs" in our hymns and endeavour to read their theology from themes such as identities, power, hybridity, cultures, and so on. This critical engagement is also geared at offering "viable critical alternatives."[4] Our focus on hymnody suggests two main lines of enquiry. Firstly, we ask about what hymns may say, questioning aspects of their language and suggesting the need to recast and revise certain elements of hymn-texts. Secondly, we interrogate how hymns are used, and in particular comment on the ambiguities of appropriating "world church" hymnody into dominant western liturgical contexts.[5]

Sounding Empire: Hymns, Theology and Imperialism

That European colonialism carried hymnody around the world and that much of European hymnody advances the cause of European colonialism should be of no surprise to readers. In *Imperialism and Music: Britain 1876–1953*, Jeffrey Richards shows how a wide range of musical forms (that includes hymns) gave expression to British National identity at home, as well as extended its reach overseas through British imperialism. Among other things, Richards shows how Victorian hymns were imperialistic, with even the masses interested in empire. His chapter on imperial hymns locates the centrality of empire and Christian militarism in a great deal of Christian song.[6]

European Christians found in what is sometimes referred to as the "Great Commission" (Matt. 28:18-20) inspiration for conquering foreign lands and their peoples. Hence, the missionaries who came out of the milieu that celebrated the expansion of European nations to the ends of the earth had no difficulty articulating that Christianity, expansion and civilization went together. Hence, mission was an opportunity for extending the Christian gospel outside England and by extension meant the expansion of the British Empire.[7] Christianizing and civilizing became euphemisms for enslavement, domination and exploitation and the theology that the established and historic churches sang underscore this. The point is this: many European ecclesial traditions – their ethos, hymns, bibles, interpretations, liturgies and doctrines – went hand in hand with the colonial enterprise to affirm production, control and domination consciously or unconsciously. Ellerton's hymn written for the Queen's jubilee (1887) sums up the tenor of the time:

> Dusky Indian, strong Australian, / Western forest, Southern sea, None are wanting, none are alien, / All in one great prayer agree– / God save the Queen!

But before him, Issac Watts (1674–1748) penned these telling lyrics:

> Sing to the Lord with joyful voice / Let every land his name adore / The British Isles shall send the noise / Across the ocean to the shore.

Our colleague John Hull has done some critical work on the hymns of Isaac Watts. While Hull does not claim to be doing so from a postcolonial perspective, his contribution falls, to an extent, within the kind of scrutiny that is in focus in this chapter. Hull underscores the fundamental point that Watt's hymnic "theology of Britain" includes among its features the identification of Britain as God's "chosen isle" and identifies the triumphant armies of the Psalms with British troops abroad. Further, Watts's tactic in his psalm "translations" is often to transfer the powers of the Hebrew monarch to Jesus and in turn to the British monarchy. At just the time at which the value of imports from India to Britain rose by at least double – the same era in which the first Christian church and the Bank of Calcutta were opened within a decade – Watts "translated" his Psalms of David:

> Before the Islands with their kings / And Europe her best tribute brings / From north and south the princes meet / To pay their homage at his feet.

> There Persia glorious to behold / There India shines in eastern golf / And barbarous nations at his word / Submit and bow and own their Lord.

Although these verses were edited out of editions of his "Psalms of David" by the nineteenth century, the legacy of empire remains even in his most durable hymns. "When I survey the wondrous cross" smacks of parallel activities of "surveying" the "glorious" "wonders" and exotic "charms" of other nations, "counting" their value and "gaining richly" from them. Although "When I survey" suggests a turning from the ultimate significance of commercial domination, the imagery of the hymn is saturated in the idea and practices of empire.[8]

A similar observation can be made of many of the hymns of Methodism. The introductory sentence in the 1933 *British Methodist Hymnbook* notes "Methodism was born in song," reflecting John Wesley's own words in the preface of *Psalms and Hymns* (1737) in which he noted that a hymnal ought to "contain all the important truths of our most holy religion," embody "experimental and practical divinity" and capture the "spirit of poetry" which becomes "the handmaid of piety."[9] No wonder scholars speak of the Methodist hymnal as embodying Methodist theology.[10] If, as Methodists claim, the theology of this particular ecclesial tradition is summed up in the hymns Methodists sing, then the hymns of the Wesleys are also worth scrutinizing as these evolved at the peak of British imperialism and the fact of their Tory mindsets. One wonders whether John Wesley's claim that the "world is my parish" is an echo of the English vision of conquering the corners of the world. And lest we forget, Charles Wesley (1707–1788) taught Methodists to sing:

> Thy sovereign grace to all extends / Immense and unconfined / From age to age it never dies / It reaches all mankind [sic].

As well as,

> O for Thy truth and mercy's sake / The purchase of Thy passion claim! / Thine heritage, the nations, take / And cause the world to know Thy name.

On the surface these words of Charles Wesley may not be speaking of empire. Indeed, Wesley may have read the moral philosophers of his time, felt convinced about the impending judgement of the world for its sins and held that Christ died for all human beings. Yet, for him, the natives in the far-flung corners of Africa had to be converted before they could be "civilized" and hence become moral beings. Moreover, he saw this as "the task thy wisdom has assigned / O let me cheerfully fulfil."[11] "With a heart full of Christ," as "ransomed servant(s)" and "docile, helpless, as a child",[12] the Wesleys saw Jesus "firing up the nations" as "soldiers of Christ, arise."[13]

The problem is that the Wesleys worked (understandably so) within the confines of a Blanco British mindset that contemplated a process that would lead to the enslaved Africans or native Americans becoming human by moving from what was termed their natural state to one of enlightenment: inculcating Christian virtues would result in this civilizing process. Those virtues were soaked with British/European values. Totally de-culturalized, a new identity would be created for the natives and the enslaved. Redeemed through Christian (British) conversion, the new creature (at last properly human) would become a more manageable workforce to the benefit of society, that is, the imperial treasury and its agents. And this mindset culminates in the image that all will live happily ever after in the emerging capitalist model of mutuality between landlords and tenants.[14]

It is no wonder that the hymns of Charles Wesley are steeped with the notion of submission, meekness and docility, proposed as the way of Jesus. And it is also not surprising that Methodism, especially at the latter part of the Wesleys' lives, was more missionary in orientation than emancipatory. For, in the final analysis, whether it was empire or not, the underlying premise was that of a superior group of people either ruling an inferior lot or a superior group of souls filled with chalky light bringing enlightenment to natives in their natural state of ignorance.[15]

What the foregoing underscores is that the colonial legacy pervades much Christian hymnody used in the West. And unfortunately this is not something confined to the past as many of those hymns are sung even to this day just as some of the newer ones re-inscribe the notions of empire, among other baleful things. To an extent some hymns have been sanitized to express sentiments and theology that reflect contemporary issues. Yet, many of these hymns have been sung for over 200 years, and the sentiments and thoughts they embraced were what the British took with them to India, Africa, the Caribbean and the dominions. Globalization today is ensuring the perpetuation of these sentiments and even if Christianity is growing in lands of the "south," many of the hymns that are sung in these places, as a result of years without any critical scrutiny of the inherited Euro-centric versions of Christianity, have remained untouched in terms of the theological notions that they espouse. As one stark example, one of us (Stephen) remembers singing hymns from Sankey and Moody's "Sacred Songs and Solos" as one of only two White members of a congregation (the other being the "imported" preacher) in a remote Aboriginal community in central Queensland. The "Aboriginal Inland Mission" congregation used this hymnal as recipients of a legacy of earlier missionary activity closely allied to lamentable forms of imperialism.

Hymns, Hymnals and their Revision: A Postcolonial Gaze

A number of questions may rightly be asked: For instance, why this harping back to those hymns written during a particular era? Are we not constantly revising our hymns and hymnals adding newer ones that reflect contemporary sentiments? Do modern hymn writers operate with notions of empire and imperial grandeur? These are pertinent questions and to them we now turn as we attempt a brief tour of some of the post-Reformation history of hymn writing and a closer scrutiny of the revising of hymnals.

Hymnals and Hymns: A Brief Overview

Hymns and hymn singing have a long and interesting history. In the western world, the Protestant Reformation played a significant role in the development of hymns and congregational hymn singing.[16] On the English landscape the person most closely associated with the development of English hymns is Isaac Watts (1674–1748), with his first hymnal appearing in 1707. Watts wrote over six hundred hymns. After him, came perhaps the greatest hymn writer of all time, Charles Wesley (1707–1788) who wrote approximately 6,500 hymns. Hymns, for some, have the ability to transgress boundaries of gender, generation, ethnicity and class.[17] For others, hymns are our "confessional documents" serving as the "container" of and formative influence on much of our faith. Hence, Albert van den Heuvel wrote: "tell me what you sing, and I'll tell you who you are."[18] Indeed, hymns do not simply lie on the page as empty words; they come to life because they are sounded and what is sounded is never value free. What they represent is linked to some agenda. Hymns were and are used to convey theological notions and teachings of the Christian faith. And hymn writers are historically, culturally and socially located: they write according to particular doctrinal viewpoints and their views reflect their time and contexts (as we have seen in relation to Watts and the Wesleys). Significantly, many hymn writers whose works are still sung lived and wrote during the high noon of European, and for our purposes British, colonial expansion. In fact, it was during this period that what we have inherited as hymnodies rapidly evolved. As such they need to be interrogated for their ideological content.[19] Here the issue of representation in hymns becomes a critical one. Who is representing whom, what is being represented and how do these representations reinforce systems of inequalities and subordination and the sustaining of colonial and neo-colonial projects. These critical questions in the process of inter-rogating our hymns (past and present).

Scrutinizing the Revision of Hymns and Hymnals: Examples and Questions

As we noted, the concern may rightly be raised as to the value of such an exercise given that our hymns and hymnbooks are constantly

being revised. Indeed, we no longer sing about the rich in the grand
hall of their castle, the poor below at their gates and that God made
them that way and ordered their state. But do we ever question
what the singing of those songs for generations has done to our
Christian ethos, doctrines and theology? What is the link with such
theology and some of the newer hymns of the "prosperity gospel"
sort that creep into our hymnals and worship (whatever the cultural
garb)? Sugirtharajah reminds us that in the minds of "most European
theologians at the time, the empire was a matter of divine dispen-
sation, and, as such, beyond ultimate criticism."[20] Furthermore, many
of our ecclesial traditions find it much safer to hold on to narrow
and rigid frameworks as these are supposed to "keep their doctrines
intact" and "their institutions safe."[21] This may be one reason why
a contemporary hymn writer such as Ruth Duck, a leader in the
revision of hymns with a view to the significance of gender, writes
that her "emphasis is on recreation, not critique of tradition." This
is a comment that relates to others appearing in a number of the
prefaces of revised hymnals. Because critical theological scrutiny is
risky, it may require a revision of beliefs, deconstructing/dismantling
of tradition and reconfiguring of identity.[22] The prefaces of some of
the newer hymnals make interesting reading, especially in terms of
their comments on the revision processes employed, the over-riding
leitmotiv and the lenses through which these have been read and
carried out.[23] We commend some of these, such as the United
Church of Christ's *New Century Hymnal* (1995), in which

> [e]very effort was made to ensure that all hymns speak to and for all God's
> people, equally. This resulted in the examination of language from racial,
> ethnic, and socio-cultural perspectives, and the review of language that
> could be diminishing to people with physical disabilities. Consideration
> was also given to imagery to assure that relate to the scientific under-
> standings of a coming generation.[24]

However, what is largely and too often passed over in the revision
processes is the connection between hymns, the colonial agenda and
empire language (past and present) and the possible implications of
this paucity of critical scrutiny of the theology, the militaristic/trium-
phalistic language and tone, cultural arrogance/superiority and the
continuing perpetuation of hegemonic notions. Pete Ward's critical
evaluations of recent generations of the "choruses" that emerged in

evangelical and charismatic circles but now traverse many church-styles includes an important critique of increasingly prevalent militaristic imagery, and needs to be applied not only to the maturing genre of the chorus but also to the wide breadth of inherited hymnody.[25] The revision of hymnbooks and the development of new styles of Christian song are both yet to engage properly with tools such as the postcolonial optic as one of the lenses through which to scrutinize how and what we sing of the faith. For if, as John Bell notes (in a similar comment to that of Albert van den Heuvel cited earlier), "congregational singing is an identity-shaping activity," and that our communities are defined "by the songs that we sing,"[26] surely hymnwriters and hymnal revisers need to ask hard questions around whose and what kind of identities and who does the defining and for whom. Of course, it may be that this is not the kind of scrutiny that hymnody committees and hymn writers are interested in. And to be fair to John Bell, he does go on to express his dismay over the multiplicity of images related to soldiers, warriors and a "tamed" Christ in our hymns, including modern ones. Bell bemoans the lack of words such as "midwives," "kitchen" and "economics." What Bell misses, however, is how many hymns may not have used a word like economics, but were shaped under colonial influences by a certain kind of "economics" that was supposed to give Europeans the God-given right to discover and exploit distant isles and lands under the pretence of bringing natives "light" while exploiting the resources of these lands. Economics was very central in Livingstone's three Cs – Civilization, Commerce and Christianity.

But let us delve some more into the subject of revision and the optics through which hymnal revision has been engaged. Obviously, the editors of *The New English Hymnal* (much used in some English Anglican settings), even in its 14th impression of 2002, never thought of the postcolonial optic informing their task and indeed saw it fitting to retain four hundred of the six hundred and fifty-six hymns printed in the original version (1906). Likewise, the editors of the United Reformed Church's *Rejoice and Sing* (1991), while revising hymns to be gender inclusive, never bothered to scrutinize the hymns of Isaac Watts and the others for their imperial overtones and connections with British imperial history. In their view, its hymns "enabled congregations to express together their worship and praise, their wonder at the almighty power and grace of God."[27] Hence, the diverse and multi-cultural nature of these congregations and the implications of Watts's link with British imperial history lay buried in the pages of the hymnal.

Should we then be surprised that during his 1997 election campaign, Tony Blair, heavily influenced by a British Christian ethos, could say that he was a proud British patriot[28] and in another address at the Lord's Mayor banquet articulated his vision for Britain and the world by noting how proud he was of British history, and the fact that Britain had an empire which should propel the nation to a more active global view and role.[29] Presently, we are trying to pick up the pieces in Afghanistan and Iraq as a result of such patriotism. George W. Bush, his "com*patriot*," is even more blatant by entitling his memoirs *Charge to Keep*, the title of which is a phrase taken from a well-known hymn by Charles Wesley. Bush's favourite hymn speaks of the charge in terms of "a God to glorify" – not about an empire to build by annexation – but Bush is not so far away from the high "churchmanship" and Tory mindset of the Wesleys – a mindset that relished certainty of a God-given right to bring the gospel to the dumb heathens!

Perhaps most interesting is *Hymns Ancient and Modern* (revised, 1981), in the preface of which the Proprietors ("a body of Church of England clergymen") noted the significant place of their hymnal as "something of a national institution" and that their revision was intended at "preserving the general tone and character which the book has always had."[30] Hence, while some alterations have been made, the intention is that the hymnal will not break "fresh ground or explore novel ideas" but that the revision "will find the same endearing and enduring qualities as in the old" and very much "in keeping with English Christianity."[31] These are interesting lines: Is there a yearning here to return to what is supposed to be some supposed "pure" state of English Christianity? What or whose version of English Christianity did these proprietors in 1981 work with? With the presence of peoples from former colonies, newer migrants in England and the engagement with other cultures and religions, certainly English Christianity needs to be re-defined and perhaps draw more on the "hybridity" and multicultural nature that has in reality always been part of its story, albeit not always told. As Sugirtharajah reminds us:

> In an ever-increasing multicultural society like ours, where traditions, histories and texts commingle, interface, a quest for unalloyed pure native roots could prove not only to be elusive but also to be dangerous.[32]

Common Praise (2000), the new edition of *Hymns Ancient and Modern* (first published in 1860–61 and since then used throughout Britain and its colonies) is also both a national and imperial text. Yet the committee responsible for its revision, while noting all the significant historical developments since the hymnal's birth, fail to mention the relationship between the hymns and British imperialism, despite the fact that during the period through which this hymnal evolved, "empire was central to English domestic life and popular consciousness."[33] While it was noted that the church has become more ecumenical, there was not a word about the *Windrush* generation and how the churches have become more multicultural. And, while the committee has attended to the archaisms of some hymns and the problematic related to gender-inclusive language, the editorial policy was intentionally "conservative," "respecting the integrity of the text, the author's known intentions, and the poetry of the original."[34]

What is interesting about these reasons is that they serve to remove any attempt to critically scrutinize hymns and the ideology that may have influenced the hymn writer. From a postcolonial stance one will want to ask why "conserve" even good poetry when the integrity of a text may be questionable because of its implicit or explicit arrogance, marginalization of peoples or groups and the locating of Euro-centric Christianity above all else (especially that which is native). Take, for example, the hymn "Dear Lord and Father of Mankind" by John Greenleaf Whittier (1807–1892). This hymn reacts to a practice in Hindu worship in which the Vedic priests consume a drink (soma) for a deep religious experience with the Divine. Finding such a practice repulsive, especially its aspect of religious frenzy, Whittier, a calm Quaker, responds to this Hindu practice by asking the God of Jesus to forgive such foolish ways and replace them with higher religious devotion characterized by "quietness," "purity," "order," "deeper reverence," and "simple trust." Certainly, the integrity of text and intentions of the author should be respected; yet the influence of this hymn – sung for generations – on the psyche of people cannot be imagined to be value free for the author, in its uses, or in terms of how readers may perceive the hymn. The intentions of a hymn writer (known or unknown) are complex because writers are always socially, culturally and politically located. Within the colonial mindset, Whittier's hymn – like many others – "offered a simple choice between truth and falsehood"; in other words, "if one is right, the other is invariably wrong." Counter to this, a postcolonial optic will not offer a forced choice "between truth and truth" nor give agency to one perspective by negating the other.[35] The fact that hymns significantly shape our identity and define who we are (as noted earlier) means they are not neutral. And this shaping can be either positive or negative. Hence, the need to interrogate hymns – not merely engage in singing poetic lines.

Even so, the generally more inclusive *Common Ground* (1998) never thought of slapping imperial overtones as one of its restrictions to determine whether hymns would find its way into this hymnbook "for all the churches." In fact, readers are told that *Common Ground* is a "unique" publication, as it "takes over 20% of its material from nations in the southern hemisphere."[36] Perhaps, this should read more like "hijacking over 20%," as the naming or representing of this transaction as "world church music" is one given by the West for music "taken" from the southern hemisphere and often sold for a neat sum. Is this a case of "expanding markets and securing new clients"?[37]

As part of this, there are important questions to be asked in relation to western churches copyrighting materials that have emerged from other cultures, which may amount to another form of exploitation and neo-colonialism.[38] Certainly, one can ask: how different is this from buying up fruits cheaply from all over the former colonies and then processing them and repackaging them either as dried fruits or canned to be exported back to these countries for prices that the natives themselves cannot afford? This is not to even mention how unrecognizable and tasteless the thing has become! One of us (Michael) recalls attending a conference where a hymn writer/musician was teaching new world songs/music to a group of ministers. Among the participants was a Ghanaian minister who protested that he could not recognize the way the song (which originated from his country of birth) was sung – much to the displeasure of the leader. This was a clear case of using "world church" hymns without appropriating concerns of context from which they come and sensitivity to people of those contexts who are now part of western communities.

One therefore wonders about the view that the inclusion of "world church music" affirms that our churches have become more inclusive, multicultural and global. Indeed, one needs to interrogate all the rhetoric surrounding multiculturalism. This would suggest it is "a project of the colonizing, dominant culture … a monocultural Anglo version of multiculturalism that wants to host, invite, and include" or incorporate "the other in 'otherwise Anglo realities and structures'."[39] The question of when inculturation and the appropriation of other people's songs and music becomes another form of exploitation or a new kind of colonialism is a very important one, not least because imperialism finds interesting ways to re-clothe itself so that we need to be ever vigilant. Here the concern of Myke Johnsont (writing in a different context, that of the cultural appropriation of Native American symbols and ceremonies) remains valid: Johnsont raises the question of "cultural appropriation" as a "form of racism" and a "weapon in the process of colonization" – especially in the context of the powerful and powerless.[40] Our concern does not lead us to the view that music and hymns should not be shared: we live in too complex a world in which cultures and people transcend boundaries and are constantly in dialogue, and, moreover, the realities of colonialism mean that destinies are intertwined and many of us straddle multiple identities. We have no difficulty with the view expressed by Michael Hawn that a variety of musical styles and hymns from around the world can deepen worship and our understanding of the incarnation of Christ.[41] Our unease is that if we do not read such sharing through a postcolonial gaze, we may not be asking the critical questions as to how this is done, who initiates and who permits it, how it is named and how it might become accessible to all.

A further related question, borrowing from Sugirtharajah, is how much of the incorporation of the "world church hymns and music" is about "disturbing and dislodging" an imperial agenda?[42] Is it possible to grow "cultural sensitivity" and yet not experience "another culture from within"?[43] Hence the question: how can the singing of a South

African and Latin American liberation song speak to a still largely Blanco European audience whose nations thrive on cheap labour, global capital and continuing impoverishment of poorer countries and sections of people within its own border? How can "world church" words and music come alive in a transforming way and not sound patronising? There is certainly the danger, to borrow from John Witvliet, of indulging in "ethno-tourism" while safely basking in our own comfort zones![44]

Sound Theology: Some Examples of Good Practice

Notwithstanding our concerns, we are pleased to note that hymnbooks and hymns have been and are being constantly revised. We affirm the practice of bringing together new hymns by contemporary hymn writers alongside older ones, whose language and images can, when necessary, be revised. We delight that it is increasingly common for hymnbooks to be reviewed in terms of education in feminist and expansive language concerns, and we are heartened by the likes of Brian Wren's work to reconfigure notions of masculinity[45] as part of the task of raising awareness of the significance of gender, which is not only a matter of how women are portrayed. We enjoy many of the ways in which perhaps the most daring contemporary hymnal, the *New Century Hymnal*, has revised and expanded the hymnody of many contemporary Christians, and we note with particular appreciation that it includes a rare "litany of light and darkness" in which darkness is not simply associated with fear and dread:

> It is only in the darkness that we can see the splendour of the universe – blankets of stars, the solitary glowings of distant planets. It was darkness that allowed the magi to find the star that guided them to where the Christ-child lay.
> **You are with us, O God, in darkness and in light.**
>
> In the darkness of the night, desert peoples find relief from the cruel, relentless heat of the sun.
> In the blessed desert darkness, Mary and Joseph were able to flee with the infant Jesus to safety in Egypt.
> **You are with us, O God, in darkness and in light.**

In the darkness of sleep, we are soothed and restored, healed and renewed.
In the darkness of sleep, dreams rise up. God spoke to Jacob and Joseph through dreams. God is speaking still...[46]

This litany offers a counter-voice to a deep and worrying tendency in much Christian song to make uncritical correlations between light and darkness and desirable and undesirable things respectively. Like Brian Wren's "Joyful is the Darkness," inspired by the line in one of his better-known hymns, "Bring Many Names," the litany of light and darkness is among too few potential fragments of "oppositional reading" to the usual currency of the metaphor of darkness.[47] In our view, recasting light and darkness imagery is a crucial strand of developing a postcolonial voice in the hymns Christians sings, and represents a constructive challenge to be set alongside the schooling in the critical gaze we have attempted throughout this chapter.

Part Three

The Word in Liturgical Contexts

4 Contrapuntal Reading: Scripture, Lectionaries and Alternative Dynamics

Introducing the Conversation

We have already made the point that postcolonial criticism has largely so far engaged theological circles in the realm of biblical studies, with some quite recent overtures in the area of systematic theology. The Bible, however, has a life beyond academic theology and biblical studies, and Christian worship provides arguably *the* main context in which the Bible is read, engaged and performed in liturgical practices. In terms of the latter, we note that in the context of colonial history, the Bible, which was made accessible through assemblies of the church, became for colonial subjects a key text in the edification of enslaved peoples and a means to improvise and signify understandings of the colonizers. Hence, the title and theme of this Part: "the word in liturgical contexts."

The Bible in the Church

Worship is an important setting in which to consider the Bible in the course of our explorations in postcolonial approaches to liturgy. We believe that a large part of bringing the insights of postcolonial criticism to bear beyond the academy will involve looking at such criticism that can be related to how the Bible is used not only in the classroom but in assemblies or gatherings of the church and local congregations. This task is especially significant given that at least some diasporic communities, such as those of the Black Christian Diaspora, define their ecclesial identity with particular reference to the Bible. This point is made by Joe Aldred about Black Majority churches in the UK, in which he is a bishop:

> Biblical models are crucial for Black Theology in Britain because the Black Christian community, especially Black-led churches, is a biblio-centric community. Any theology, therefore, that does not engage in a primary way with biblical text will find itself *ipsofacto* [sic] divorced from the Black Church with which it seeks to engage.[1]

We take Aldred's point in its broad contours. However, we have some misgivings about his ease of use of the singular – "the Black church" – for what we know is textured ecclesial realities. We also hesitate at his suggestion that all Black churches are "biblio-centric," at least in senses that would reflect Aldred's own reading of biblical texts.

The insights of Philip Potter, Robert Beckford and Anthony Reddie can serve to underscore our suspicion of Aldred's talk of a singular "Black church," and our preference for assertion of diversity within, as well as between, Black ecclesial tradition(s). Potter, a Methodist who became General Secretary of the World Council of Churches, grounded his own theological articulations on re-readings of biblical texts, consistently noting that Black folks of the African Diaspora are "biblical realists," not literalists.[2] Hence, Potter's re-readings would typically include critical scrutiny of particular biblical texts under consideration, and as part of that those texts viewed through the optics of colonial history and the experiences of enslaved Africans. Beckford, a Black British theologian and cultural critic of Pentecostal background, evidently does affirm the centrality of the Bible for Black spirituality, yet he readily argues against a fundamentalist and literal reading of scriptures. Hence, his use of a hermeneutical strategy which he calls "dub optics" to re-read the gospels.[3] Reddie, a Black British Methodist theologian of Caribbean ancestry, also affirms the centrality of scriptures in the ecclesial life of Black Christians, yet he too goes beyond a critique of literalist and conservative approaches of biblical texts. Using narratives of transatlantic Black experiences (especially in the context of colonial history) as his departure point, Reddie critically interrogates, questions and re-reads the Bible to the extent of even giving precedence to Black experience over the Bible as the word of God.[4] Our point in invoking these exemplars is that while each of them appreciates the centrality of scriptures in the ecclesial lives of Black Christians, each in their own way, and especially when juxtaposed, underscore multiple ways that, in Aldred's terms, "biblical models" are developed, exercised and interpreted in view of integral, complementary understandings and authorities.

The significant point for us here is that Aldred seems not to wish to use a postcolonial optic to interrogate the Bible so as to be able to locate the imperial agenda in biblical texts. The others cited above can and do embrace postcolonial convictions. Each of them honours the Bible and affirms its theological importance, albeit with slightly different nuances. But the term "biblio-centric" means different things to them. So while the Bible is indeed crucial for a large body of Black British Christians of all ecclesial traditions, in terms of what we might call the dynamics of biblio-centricism, Aldred speaks for some and not all of them.

It is important to be clear, then, that many Black Christians (as other "kinds" of Christians) would certainly not mean by "bibio-centric" what Emmanuel Lartey (himself a Black Christian) points out as what is meant by "biblicism":

> In which the literal words, or else the book itself, are such sacred objects that they are taken literally and may become a legalistic battering ram used more to defeat than inspire and encourage persons.[5]

Lartey himself contests "the assumption that only literal, and not critical or contextual, readings and interpretations lead to hearing 'the word of God'." Engaging with the Bible "in a primary way," for many Black Christians and certainly for Black theology means bringing sharp questions into play with biblical texts. We see no reason to exclude from the idea of engaging the Bible in a "primary" way the kind of postcolonial approach to the texts which is demonstrated by Reddie, among others.

The Bible – a Plural Book

The word "bible" itself comes from *biblia*, a plural word meaning "books." Its plurality is, however, easily misrepresented by being bound in one volume in the way it is often handled in its canonical context or elsewhere in collections of lectionary sequences for liturgical use. The downplaying (intentional or not) of the inherent diversity within the collection (as is clearly evident in the four gospel accounts and the pastorals) has colonial overtones. As Sugirtharajah observes:

> One of the characteristics of colonial discourse is the rejection of diversity. Colonial discourse is staunchly wedded to unvarying and exclusive truth and tolerates no dissent or debate.[6]

Certainly, controlling truth under the pretext of countering heresies has been one reason that we have the Bible in its present form,[7] as well as a long proclivity towards homogenizing of the biblical stories.

Another reality we need to be aware of is related to texts which have been excluded from the collection that comprises the *biblia*. Hence, Sugirtharajah rightly observes:

> Postcolonial biblical criticism needs to expand the biblical canon and incorporate those diverse texts which were suppressed or excluded in the ecclesiastical power-game of selection and rejection.[8]

This is why scholars such as Sugirtharajah strongly contend that "canonical scriptures are not the sole conveyors of truth" and suggests the need to move "beyond the limitations of the Jewish-Hellenistic context and pay attention also to the Jewish-Aramaic" context.[9] But even in terms of the plurality already to be found in what we have as the canon, *when* its plurality can be kept in view, we have a signal reminder that the Bible does not, and can barely be expected to, communicate one core, or central, message or truth. In fact the reality of the Bible can much better be imagined as layers and complexities to "truth." The Bible envelops multiple voices, sometimes more or less in harmony with each other, yet at other points sharply divergent, even contradictory.

Lectionary Dynamics

The Revised Common Lectionary (RCL), or some modest variation of it (such as that employed in the Church of England), has become very widely used, and as such a very significant expression of ecumenism in contemporary Christianity. So the RCL is perhaps the most widely employed pan-Protestant liturgical resource, particularly, as just noted, in its having been taken up in traditions where lectionary schemes had previously been unfamiliar. And the RCL is not only important across Protestant traditions, because its ecumenical stretch is broader, having grown out of shared reflection on the Roman Catholic Church's experience of its Lectionary for Mass. For each Sunday over a three-year period, the RCL provides a reading from Hebrew scripture, a psalm, a New Testament reading and a gospel reading. The readings are always in that order – Hebrew scripture, psalm, New Testament, gospel – though the way that the four readings relate to each other varies. That is, the psalm may be related to the first (Hebrew scripture) reading, and both of these are independent of the New Testament and gospel, which are in turn not intended to be "linked" with each other. So the separate readings stand in a sequence which connects them, but into which no particular governing theme is intended to be read.[10]

Following this observation, it is important to note that ritual books in different traditions increasingly allow the sermon to be preached after any of the readings in the sequence, rather than after the final (i.e. gospel) reading, as had previously been customary in many traditions. Indeed, the same ritual books oftentimes suggest that "sermon" may be understood in a variety of ways, allowing for a range of engagements with text and context – including discussion, testimony, and various art-forms.[11] A steady feature of the lectionary dynamic is, however, that the gospel is always read last (at least *when* it is read – some traditions mandate use of gospel reading at a eucharist, while others do not). Hence, the lectionary encourages a sense of Jesus "getting the last word," with accounts of his actions, if not always his recorded words, being proposed as the principal interpretive lens at the culmination of the sequence of other texts.

In effect, a strong christological hermeneutic is proposed by the Revised Common Lectionary, which may be one of the things that has commended it to churches which had previously rejected set schemes of reading. Despite its sense of christological privilege, however, it nevertheless remains the case that to some extent at least, in lectionary chains, different Bible readings are juxtaposed to one another – according to Gordon W. Lathrop, explicitly and intentionally speaking "different – even wildly contrasting – views."[12]

Lectionary patterns can, then, be regarded as particular ways of being conscious of, and honouring, the diversity of the Bible. They resist the isolation of one text alone being held up before a congregation – least of all one drawn from the preacher's whim – and insist that one reading is heard alongside another. Readings set alongside each other provide contexts of meaning for individual pericopes proclaimed in a sequence – although that meaning is of course shaped not only by questions about what readings are included (and excluded) from the sequence, but from the order in which they are presented, framing the next, perhaps grating against the previous one, to mention just two of the most obvious possible dynamics. At least the juxtaposing of various biblical texts carries with it the potential to subvert and challenge dominant and centralized notions related to workings of the divine.

The ways in which juxtaposed texts interpret each other – different sequences enabling different interpretations – also needs to be remembered in the wider ecumenical pattern of worship which most commonly moves from word to sacrament, a shift in which the ministry of the word, focused on scripture, is juxtaposed with the "visible word" of the table (or foot-washing, or some other kind of broadly sacramental action). Gordon Lathrop, who, with Gail Ramshaw, has been one of the key liturgical theologians to present versions of lectionaries for use in Christian assembly,[13] argues that the juxtaposition of word and sacrament is a pattern learned from the Bible itself. So he suggests that:

> the truth about God … takes at least two words… In this world speaking about God with just one "word" – one connected and logical discourse for example – will almost inevitably mean speaking a distortion, even a lie. It will suggest that God is a consequent idea, not a burning fire and a mysterious presence … for us the mystery of God, for all that it may indeed be graciously present in human speech, must be proposed by triangulation. Words, even such contradictory words as "now" and "not yet" or "judgment" and "mercy" or "absence" and "presence" or "death" and "life" or "one" and "many," will necessarily be put side by side, like two candles near the altar or the two cherubim on the ark of the covenant…[14]

Yet, sacramental celebrations also propose a christological hermeneutic akin to that inherent in lectionary sequences which build up to a gospel reading in so far as sacraments, infused as they are with paschal imagery, zoom in to focus at some key point on a centripetal narrative of Christ's life, death and rising. So in word and table set alongside each other, Jesus also "gets the last word" in sacramental actions, which are themselves always juxtapositions of signs and/or movements and dominical words or deeply traditional words associated in some close way with Christ. By noting these dynamics in the context of the exploration of the lectionary, we are able to see that there are different levels of interplay between words and actions in liturgy, which at least some liturgical theologians (notably Gordon Lathrop, cited already) want to relate to intra-biblical lectionary dynamics. If this is the case, then apart from anything else, the interplay of word and sacrament is arguably one way of being "biblio-centric," à la Joe Aldred, although it may not be what Aldred had in mind. Moreover, the ways in which lectionary sequences concern readings shaping contexts for readings, and the wider liturgical dynamic they encourage, can readily be imagined as being hospitable to other contextual readings.

The kinds of juxtaposition that mark lectionary sequences influence a whole style of theological thinking, such as the "schools" within liturgical theology that are indebted to the influential lead of Gordon Lathrop. Lathrop sees the Bible – in its plurality and multivalency – as itself teaching the church theology by what he calls "triangulation" and what, elsewhere,[15] he most commonly calls "juxtaposition."[16] One of Lathrop's key points is that use of a lectionary continually holds such juxtapositions before those churches that use it to order their pathways through scripture. Lathrop's stress on the lectionary's embrace of "different," "wildly contrasting" views is especially salient to what we wish to say in later parts of this chapter.

Canonical and Lectionary Contexts

Canonical and lectionary contexts for biblical pericopes are two different ways of searching for meanings in the diverse corpus of the scriptures. A key question for us is whether understandings and practices of lectionary reading encourage the discernment of the multiple voices there to be found in the canon, or whether lectionary reading may rather represent a colonial tactic of encouraging one controlling voice. In its prescriptions for reading pathways through biblical material it is vulnerable to the charge that it bolsters one version of reading through a diverse corpus, often smoothing down what is in fact chaotic and difficult terrain. Although not a postcolonial scholar, we value the liturgist Michael Vasey's insistence on the "liberating chaos of the scriptures,"[17] itself expressing a conviction that the discordant character of the Bible may be as much gift – liberation – as problem. Indeed, we note Vasey's own attempt to re-read scriptural pericopes that had long been used as tools to define and confine the practice of homosexual persons such as himself.[18] Notwithstanding Vasey's hope of liberation in the scriptures, it remains that from a conscious postcolonial perspective the controlling reading tactics of lectionary patterns are matters that must be engaged with the like of Sugirtharajah's comments about "rejection of diversity."

In this context, Edward Said's notion of contrapuntality, drawn from musical genres, is of great merit. It works with a practice of juxtaposition, familiar in understandings of lectionary, and proposes that readings are juxtaposed with particular kinds of responses, counterpoints that reveal colonial implications of texts. Said introduced his own understanding of contrapuntality with reference to Jane Austen's *Mansfield Park*, in which protagonists within her story – the family of "Sir Thomas Bertram" – enjoy privilege in large part because Bertram owns an estate in Antigua. Their prosperity – and the noted extravagance of some members of the family (Bertram's eldest son) – depends upon morally ambiguous "overseas interests" and colonial expansion. As the exploitative dynamics of empire are not the subject of critical reflection within the novel, a contrapuntal reading of the text will involve the interspersion of counterpoints which make clear the costs of Bertram's wealth. Furthermore, Said notes that exposure of colonial dynamics within Austen's stories has not been a strong feature of literary criticism of her work, which is a further layer of complicity – through silence – in suspect imperial privilege; hence, established canons of interpretation also need to be counterpointed and challenged.[19]

Contrapuntal reading can therefore be seen to push further than the perhaps more neutral notion of juxtaposition, familiar in liturgical theology, towards a more confronting mode of engaging texts. In contrapuntal method, it is not just that one voice might stand adjacent to another; rather, contrapuntality suggests that voices do more than stand alongside each other in order. They may interject, interrupt, disrupt, upset, and contest.

We note that contrapuntality has not been a major feature of liturgical practices commended by the churches. It is, however, possible to find liturgical precedents, albeit ones about which some caution is needed. Richard Giles's handbook for "creating transformative worship throughout the year," *Times and Seasons*,[20] is the successor to his *Creating Uncommon Worship*, on "transforming the liturgy of the eucharist."[21] Both books veer from official, denominationally mandated practices – notably by commending, in an Anglican context, the practice of local assemblies writing their own eucharistic prayers. In contrast to Anglican liturgical canons, Giles asserts, "it is a sign of a healthy and mature community of faith when the assembly can set about creating a eucharistic prayer appropriate to its own story and situation"[22] – a defiance that can, of course, be harnessed in postcolonial critique of ecclesial authorities' proclivities to control. In *Times and Seasons*, Giles proposes an alternative to a carol service, "Not a Carol Service: A Non-Liturgical Service in Advent." It suggests use of well-known carols such as "O Come All Ye Faithful" and "While Shepherds Watched," though the apparently well-worn pattern of Advent celebration involves a surprise:

> During this hymn, the service is interrupted by a member of the faith community acting the part of an amiable drunk who engages the worship leader in an exchange about the meaning of what is going on.
> The drunk ushers in his heavily pregnant girlfriend. They have nowhere to sleep that night; consternation, embarrassment.
> Not knowing what to do, the organist strikes up "Away in a manger" and the congregation manages a few lines before the drunk interrupts again, demanding attention and help.
> The worship leader invites the young couple to come up and sit beside him/her, and suggests the assembly listen to a story.[23]

The story which is then read is not from the Advent sequence of gospel infancy narratives, but rather the parable of the Good Samaritan from Lk. 10.29-37. The romanticizing reference to "amiable drunk" and other stereotypes notwithstanding, there are things to commend in this gentle subversion of expectations of Advent carol services. Strength of commendation might depend much on what is made of exposition of the Good Samaritan story – itself ripe for postcolonial interpretation that evokes self-awareness and practical solidarity. Nevertheless the emphasis on interruption, and demand for attention and help – albeit here staged – perhaps open up a pathway from familiar expectations of liturgical events towards the possibility of more spontaneous, risky counterpoint.

If the biblical canon as a whole, and particular pericopes on their own and in manifold intra-biblical juxtapositions, are intertwined with the history of western European hegemony, should not canonical and lectionary contexts and contents be explored from the perspectives of both colonizer and colonized? And should not the colonized interrupt the ordered readings of colonizers, and those who inherit the colonizers' privilege? Said's notion of contrapuntal reading proposes ways of engaging both imperialism and resistance to it by commending that texts are considered so as to open up imperial proclivities, which involves listening to how the texts are read, heard and perhaps resisted, by different kinds of respondees. So Said suggests some significant ways of developing postcolonial scrutiny of the use of lectionaries.

Whereas the postcolonial engagements with the Bible conducted in the academy may be conscious of the Bible in its canonical shape (even if not prioritizing that configuration of its various materials), the lectionary sequences within the shape of Christian worship in many ecclesial traditions do not seem as yet to have been engaged with. We need also to note that not all Christians follow a lectionary, let alone the same one. It is most likely that some of those for whom Joe Aldred speaks in Black British Pentecostal Churches are one case in point. But it remains that shared lectionary patterns are coming to be embraced by an ever-wider circle of ecclesial traditions, including some that had previously eschewed set patterns of readings, preferring to think that readers and/or preachers might better lean into the leading of the Spirit, perhaps. So, although their "commendation" is clearly weaker than traditions which mandate use of lectionaries (such as the Church of England), the British Methodist Church now commends use of the ecumenical Revised Common Lectionary, as do the Baptist Union of Great Britain and the United Reformed Church. We acknowledge the ecumenical significance of such developments, and we wish to invite ecumenical attention to problems – resistance to diversity, the smothering of subaltern voices, witting or unwitting colonization, and so on – that may in fact be bolstered by such gains. At the very least, a postcolonial perspective on lectionary patterns as important features of Christian worship will wish to demand that both users of lectionaries and the contents of lectionaries themselves are beyond naïvety about what kinds of power they may shelter and sustain.

"Deviations" from Lectionary Sequences

Having outlined the above, we now search for constructive ways of both engaging and contesting particular lectionary dynamics. We begin by noting that it is not always appreciated how much freedom to depart from set or suggested readings (at least at certain times of the year – in fact the most part of it) is granted in some traditions that employ lectionaries. The Church of England is a case in point, which although stressing that "authorized lectionary provision [is] not matter for local decision except where that provision permits,"[24] permits wide variation. *Common Worship* outlines the rule that during the Christmas cycle (from Advent Sunday through to Candlemas) and the Easter cycle (from Ash Wednesday through to Pentecost) and on Trinity Sunday and All Saints Day, the prescribed readings must be used.[25] However, outside those times – all of "ordinary time" and, therefore, a majority of each year – local lectionaries may be produced "for pastoral reasons or preaching or teaching purposes."[26] The point about departure is important, because it highlights permissions – if they are needed – to engage explicitly postcolonial approaches, among others. In what follows, we want to encourage engagement with such permission, while at the same time also voicing critical concerns about the lectionary such that we do not wish simply to commend a compliant "playing by its rules."

Dynamics of Power

Both canon and lectionary were composed by north Atlantic persons, largely White males, and often with ecclesiastical function – and power, such as those who authorize ritual books for use by others.[27] In the compilation of lectionary chains, no matter what claims are made about the independence and autonomy of one reading in relation to another, many important decisions are and must be made about what parts of the Bible are included in the lectionary (parts of the *Epistle of James* and so much of the *Song of Songs* are notable exclusions from the RCL), which reading is heard next to another, and in what order.

The compilers of lectionaries are therefore powerful, to put it mildly. One of the most obvious assertions of power is in the way that the lectionary is organized around the liturgical year which reflects the natural seasons of the northern hemisphere, and which is consequently deeply out of kilter with experience across the southern hemisphere, where the majority of the world's Christians are located, and to where it is commonly said the "weight of gravity" of Christianity in the twenty-first century has/is shifted/ing. In this sense the lectionary confirms the "normalcy" of European and North Atlantic Christians while provoking a considerable sense of dissonance for many in the global south.[28]

In galvanizing a calendar organized in relation to natural seasons, the lectionary of course to some extent simply mirrors the particular circumstances of the environment in which divine incarnation is alleged: Jesus was born in the northern hemisphere, and the church's proclamation, at first more locally, and over time further afield, might naturally draw on the realm of experience open to persons in the north. Still, apart from wishing to question why symbols (from the natural cycles of times, or anything else) should continue to be drawn primarily from the north, a postcolonial optic on the lectionary will also wish to revisit why early churches' "inculturation" of the calendar entailed outright contest with both Jewish and pagan religious traditions, as awareness of the origins of key festivals such as Easter and Christmas makes plain to be the case. Dynamics of super-cession, superiority, disregard and renunciation are inscribed in the origins of the Christian calendar, and are arguably re-inscribed by contemporary use of a lectionary developed primarily in the north.

Challenging Lectionaries: Postcolonial Reading Strategies

In our conversation thus far, we have already hinted at the ways that when viewed via a postcolonial optic, how lectionaries' dynamics can be both challenged and at the same time offer vistas for a constructive conversation. We have also seen that while lectionaries offer a diversity of readings from a multiplicity of biblical voices and theological positions, there is a tendency towards a christological bias, a bias towards the seasonal cycles of the northern hemisphere and power dynamics that favour a particular group (geographical, ecclesial and gendered). Certainly, one cannot rule out the possibilities of homogenizing and controlling proclivities in lectionary selection and interpretations, in spite of the "deviations" from lectionary sequences.

Mindful that lectionaries and their constitutive pericopes are not value-free aspects of the liturgical life of ecclesial communities, a postcolonial perspective opens up possibilities for a necessary critical conversation. How, for instance, can we locate colonial tendencies and entanglements in our lectionary and pericope readings? And how have imperial practices and hegemonic tendencies shaped these? As we have already hinted, this may very well happen due to the ways these are put together and the agendas of those responsible for this task. It may also be pertinent to contemplate the reasons for lectionaries, or indeed any other pattern of reading, in the performance of Christian liturgy. We would suggest that postcolonial optics can serve as a tool "to detect oppression, expose misrepresentation," and to "promote a fairer world" to borrow from Sugirtharajah.[29]

In arranging lectionary readings, ecclesiastical authorities do not seem to engage as a major concern the problematics related to biblical narratives and the texts of the biblical canon. Understandably, this is not their focus in compiling "readings for the assembly," and yet we would assert that promoting a fairer world certainly ought to be within the orbit of concern of ecclesial groups. We would urge from a postcolonial perspective that in future lectionary revision such a concern is both explicitly stated and efforts to enact it explained, for unstated, any appeal to authority and faithfulness in lectionary compilation is likely to reflect the interesting relationship with hegemonic proclivities to control and shut down debate and dissent found within the scriptures themselves as well as canonical compilation.[30]

What a postcolonial scrutiny will insist on and demonstrate is that any such selection cannot be neutral. There is always an interest at stake. Thus, by assigning texts to be read on specific feast days and through significant seasons of the church, ecclesiastical authorities and their representatives do in fact make theological judgments in their selection (and editing) of readings and how they group these in terms of their understanding of the liturgical seasons and feasts. Evaluating these selections and the reading/interpreting of these texts through a postcolonial optic will raise critical questions about any tendency, whatever the theological or hermeneutical colour, that gives the Bible the unquestioned benefit of the doubt as *the* only place where answers for critical and urgent questions facing humankind today, where God has spoken with finality and where liberation and hope, can be found.[31] In other words a postcolonial reading will not only give agency to a multiplicity of voices in terms of these and other issues: it will also highlight that the Bible is a complex and problematic textual repository that embodies the historical, socio-political and cultural complexities not only of its own world, but that of the shapers of what we presently have as an acceptable canon and pattern of proclamation and interpretation. From a postcolonial perspective, one key question for future conversations on lectionaries will be around ways to "expand the biblical canon and incorporate those diverse texts which were suppressed or excluded in the ecclesiastical power-game of selection and rejection."[32]

In a previous section we noted the possibility of "deviations" in lectionary sequencing. Perhaps this can open up opportunities for the use of non-canonical biblical texts. Deviations, on the other hand, will sit very well within the postcolonial agenda, as it offers opportunities for praxiological impulses that can give shape to theological and liturgical dissent, and the subverting of totalizing tendencies geared at restricting theology, rituals and practices. In this regard, the postcolonial strategy of textual juxtapositions and contrapuntal reading become a necessary strategy and habit to nurture and employ. We wish to highlight and borrow from Edward Said's contributions with regard to the ways one should read a literary text that takes into account intertwined histories and perspectives. This strategy does offer possibilities of how we can juxtapose, read and interpret lectionary readings. For Said, contrapuntal analysis or counterpoint reading functions on the premise that there is a multiplicity of voices at play that may appear as an organized whole, but with only a provisional privileging allowed to any one voice. In our specific case, the gospel reading may be last, but this method would not see this as Jesus having the last word or even point to a rigid christological bias. It will certainly want to juxtapose the Pauline tendencies towards universalizing the gospel (and in the process neutralize ethnic and cultural differences) and that of the Galilean/Palestinian Jew, Jesus, whose mission and ministry was configured and reconfigured within a Jewish religious framework.

Postcolonial optics, via contrapuntal reading, will be largely concerned with reading strategies and interpretations. Their concern will be to interpret different perspectives simultaneously while trying to see how the text interacts with a lectionary chain as well as with historical, biographical and socio-political contexts. Reading will be done with an awareness of the many ideological interests in the text, including the ways they have been juxtaposed, the canonizing of scriptures and the link between the history of the Christian church and empires. Hence, what is *not* said may be just as important as what is said; and what went into the readings is as important as what the author excluded.

Further, there are also other ways in which contrapuntality or counterpoint may take on creative possibilities. One such opportunity is one that will encourage suitable interruptions, challenge, contesting and argument in the liturgy. As Surgitharajah puts it in the context of hermeneutics: "[t]he interpreter has not only a discursive function but also an interventionist one which is ethically and ideologically committed."[33] It may be that opportunities can be created to allow counterpoints, interventions and interruptions from apocryphal readings and from popular readings of marginalized groups (for instance asylum seekers, aboriginal peoples etc.) whose voices are rarely given agency in our liturgies.

We close by drawing attention to two particular writings which make constructive contributions to postcolonial reading of the Bible in Christian assemblies. Firstly, we note Jione Havea's call for a "Commoner's Lectionary" that will both complement and contest the Common Lectionary.[34] Havea's essay is a contextualized or *sited* example (in his case, especially relating to the Pacific Islands) of how the "commonness" of lectionary schemes which purport to be common ones can begin to be challenged and unravelled. In "attempting to rescue the RCL from the colonial legacy," Havea suggests the need

> to give attention to the traditions, experiences and the reasonings of commoners. There are two interconnected moves here: critique the mainline (hermeneutics of suspicion) and make room for the sidelined (hermeneutics of identification and of retrieval).

He is aware that this would evoke both "growling sighs from the dominant classes, who will loathe the questioning of their mainline ways" as well as "sighs of release from sidelined commoners, who will rejoice in their recognition." The Commoners' Lectionary in Havea's imagination would be biased towards local readers or more appropriately "tellers," and amongst other things would consider

> *biblical texts* (from different slants), *other ancient texts* (e.g. selections on hospitality and care for the outsider or stranger taken from the Vedas, Qur'an, Talmud or church fathers and mothers), *local instructions* (in the form of stories, dances, riddles, proverbs or legends), and *recent popular texts* (e.g. novels, artwork, craft, lyrics and movies).

Alongside the kind of approach commended by Havea, the work of someone like David Joy can provide important impetus for postcolonial reading of the Bible in the assembly of the church. Joy's work, "a hermeneutical paradigm for a postcolonial context,"[35] specifically his own India, carefully sets the Gospel of Mark in multiple overlapping contexts, including the history of western scholarship, its deployment in colonial missionary endeavour and particular subaltern readings – such as that by Dalit persons. More than this, however, he exposes colonial powers and what he evocatively calls "imperial scars" within the Markan material itself. Both the voices of oppressors and the pervasiveness of the poor within the gospel are identified, and subaltern presence within the Markan narratives is especially lifted up. Readings of particular Markan texts are offered through the lenses of race, gender, nationhood and their inter-twining in hybrid forms. The colonized context in which "Mark" writes, as well as colonizing dynamics of later interpretations, are foregrounded.

In our view, the biblical scholarship represented by Havea and Joy is the kind that needs to be engaged in Christian assembly. Such scholarship is invaluable for the critique and conversation we wish to encourage and crucial to postcolonial perspectives being expanded beyond the confines of the academy.

Part Four

Time, Space and Persons

5 Time and Space: The Festival of Lessons and Carols

Introducing the Conversation

As ordained ministers who have served in Lutheran, Reformed and Anglican ecclesial traditions, we have over the years led and participated in the annual "Festival of Lessons and Carols." Over the span of these years, in our rethinking of this service through liberation and postcolonial optics, we have grown uncomfortable with the premise and various aspects of this service. We find ourselves in agreement with the view that the Festival of Lessons and Carols is grounded "on a fundamentally flawed theological concept," one that reinforces a narrow and uninformed attitude towards biblical texts.[1]

We contend that the service centres on a misreading of the Hebrew scriptures and that its hymnody amplifies many problematic notions. We agree with John Selby Spong that this must change. Spong goes on to express the view that "[l]iturgists with a commitment to scholarship and with an eye to the future need to develop ... a new form for this beautiful service."[2] We have both an eye to the present and the future and a commitment to scholarship, and what we offer in this chapter are some of our concerns related to revising the shape and content of this particular liturgy. Our thoughts are located through the postcolonial optic as noted, defined and explained in the introduction and employed in all the other preceding chapters.

A Brief History of the Service

The Service of Nine Lessons and Carols has its origins in an order crafted in 1880 for use in Truro Cathedral by the then Bishop of

Truro, Edward Benson. In 1918, Eric Milner-White, the then Dean of King's College, Cambridge, adopted and expanded the service for use there. Over time, it has meandered its way into the liturgies and worship practices of various Christian traditions, and not least secured a place in the current official liturgical resources for the Church of England, where material from the Truro/Cambridge festival forms the heart of "Carol Services in the Christmas Season" in *Common Worship: Times and Seasons*.[3] More significantly, the service has been broadcast every year but one (1930) since 1928; from the early 1930s it has in fact been transmitted overseas by the BBC to apparent audiences of millions across the world, and recordings of the service are widely available on vinyl or CD. Kings College suggest that

> In these and other ways the service has become public property. From time to time the College receives copies of services held, for example, in the West Indies or the Far East, and these show how widely the tradition has spread. The broadcasts, too, have become part of Christmas for many far from Cambridge. One correspondent writes that he heard the service in a tent on the foothills of Everest; another, in the desert. Many listen at home, busy about their own preparations for Christmas. Visitors from all over the world are heard to identify the Chapel as "the place where the Carols are sung."[4]

In these ways, the service has come to enjoy international attention, even iconic status, for suggesting something of quintessential "Anglican" worship, even perhaps characteristics of "Englishness," that is, it may be regarded as one of what David Isihoro calls "a collection of stereotypes."[5] *Times and Seasons* states that "the festival of Lessons and Carols is itself an influential English creation of the late nineteenth century, made widespread by the choir of King's College, Cambridge…"[6] At least in its performance at King's College, we are proudly informed that "the backbone of the service, the lessons and the prayers, has remained virtually unchanged"[7] since its introduction in 1918, even if some of the hymns have changed over time. One constant feature of the service's hymnody has, however, been the use of "Once in Royal David's City" as the opening carol.

The Colonial Context

E. W. Benson composed the Service of Lessons and Carols for use in what was at the time a "wooden shed, which then served as his cathedral in Truro."[8] While "his" cathedral was being built, the discourse on the abolition of slavery in the colonies was in full swing and India was formally taken over from East India Company and ruled by the British Raj. Perhaps the cathedral in Truro was built with the help of benefactors such as those who made a fortune through the transatlantic slave trade, plantations in the colonies and the East India Company. By the time Eric Milner-White took up the Service for use in Cambridge, Rudyard Kipling who penned his famous "White Man's Burden"[9] had published Kim[10] and the British Empire embraced almost one quarter of the earth's territory and over four hundred million people. Linked to the expansion and consolidation of the British Empire were a flurry of missionary activities. Missionaries may have sometimes been critical of colonial practices, yet they were unable "to sever altogether their connection to British imperial power." For located on the "the frontline of the colonial encounter" missionaries can be thought of as the storm-troopers of "imperialism's cultural assault on indigenous subjectivities" or the "colonizers of consciousness."[11]

As reference to Kipling suggests, the British literary scene and the literature produced during this period make very interesting reading, especially their representation of the colonies, the colonized, their cultures, religions and texts. These would have had a significant influence on both Benson and Milner-White. For as the late Edward Said noted: "nearly everywhere in nineteenth and early twentieth-century British culture" one can locate an abundance of "allusions to the facts of empire" and nowhere more than the British novel in terms of "regularity and frequency." Viewed as a whole, this is what Said refers to as "a structure of attitude and reference."[12]

Quite obviously, the service developed in the prime and high noon of colonial expansion. As far as we are aware, this sort of connection has not been made specifically with regard to this liturgy, even though "empire did loom large in the minds of many Britons."[13] J. Cain and A. J. Hopkins remind us:

Imperialism … was neither an adjunct to British history nor an expression of a particular phase of its industrial development but an integral part of the configuration of British society, which it both reinforced and expressed.[14]

Indeed, as Susan Thorne contends: "British men and women from all walks of life were connected by many and powerful ties to their nations' expanding empire."[15] Empire's consequences have a long reach: it "was not a singular place, but a set of geographical and cultural spaces." Edouard Glissant pushes this further by contending that "[t]he west is not in the West. It is a project, not a place."[16] Empire manifested itself in enterprises, for example, the slave trade, indentured servitude, plantation economy, East and West India Companies and in socio-cultural-religious appendages (foreign missions, zenana teacher training societies, British and Foreign Bible Society). Significantly, "colonial subjects were everywhere in European culture at home."[17] Hence, our scrutiny of the service subjects it to a postcolonial reading in order to expose its colonial alliances and critique its continued and flawed colonial resonances.

Locating Milner-White's Contribution

One of Milner-White's contributions to the evolution of the service was his bidding prayer in 1901:

> Beloved in Christ, be it this Christmastide our care and delight to hear again the message of the angels, and in heart and mind to go even unto Bethlehem and see this thing which is come to pass, and the Babe lying in a manger. Therefore let us read and mark in Holy Scripture the tale of the loving purposes of God from the first days of our disobedience unto the glorious redemption brought to us by this Holy Child.
> But first, let us pray for the needs of the whole world; for peace on earth and goodwill among all his people; for unity and brotherhood within the Church he came to build, and especially in this city [town, village] of … and diocese of … And because this of all things would rejoice his heart, let us remember, in his name, the poor and helpless, the cold, the hungry and the oppressed; the sick and them that mourn, the lonely and unloved, the aged and the little children; all those who know not the Lord Jesus, or who love him not, or who by sin have grieved his heart of love. Lastly, let us remember before God all those who rejoice with us,

but upon another shore, and in a greater light, that multitude which no man can number, whose hope in the Word made flesh, and with whom in the Lord Jesus we are forever one.[18]

We should note in these paragraphs not only that Milner-White's gendered language for humankind has not been inclusivized in *Times and Seasons*, but also that its images of "another shore," gradations of "light," "lordship," and the idea that others "know not the Lord Jesus" would reverberate deeply with the colonialist rhetoric of his era. The difficulties of Christian feminists in ascribing "lordship" to Jesus, or anyone else, are well rehearsed; awareness of the image's resonance with colonial oppression might now invite fresh attention to the question of a moratorium on its use, or at least continued – reinvigorated – struggle to find alternative metaphors.[19]

(Mis)reading the Scriptures

The "nine lessons"[20] proposed by the King's College service were as follows:

1. Genesis 3:8-14 (The Fall)
2. Genesis 22:1-19 or 22:15-18 (The promise to Abraham)
3. Isaiah 9:2, 6, 7 (The prophecy of the Messiah's birth)
4. Isaiah 11:1-9 (The prophecy of the Messiah's kingdom of peace) or Micah 5:2-4 (The Messiah will be born in Bethlehem)
5. Luke 1:26-38 (The Annunciation to Mary) or Isaiah 60:1-6, 19 (The coming of the glory of the Lord)
6. Matthew 1:18-23 (The birth of Emmanuel) or Luke 2:1-7 (The birth of Jesus)
7. Luke 2:8-16 (The shepherds go to the manger)
8. Matthew 2:1-11 (The magi are led by the star to Jesus)
9. John 1:1-14 (The Incarnation of the Word of God)

In its provisions for "Carol Services in the Christmas Season," *Times and Seasons* also offers two alternative sequences of readings alongside the pattern from King's College: one falls under the heading "Good news for the poor," which is said to be "also suitable for Christmas Eve"[21] and which intersperses seven readings with extracts from

Psalms. Of the seven readings, five are from the Hebrew scriptures and the final two come from a Christian epistle (Phil. 2:5-11 – interestingly in our context, "he took the form of a servant…") and a gospel reading – either Luke 1:26-38 or 2:1-20 depending on whether the sequence is read at a service in Advent or Christmas – interspersed with the *Magnificat*.[22] Notably, the *Magnificat* is another text that feminists have demanded be subject to a moratorium.[23] The other sequence of readings in *Times and Seasons* is headed "The Gospel of Luke," a sequential pathway through the Lucan infancy narrative culminating in a final reading from Titus – either 2:11-14 or 3:3-7: "The Grace of God has appeared for the salvation of all."[24]

These alternatives to the "nine tiny lessons"[25] of the King's College service may raise questions of the Truro/Cambridge sequence, although in our view they are themselves still riddled with the difficulty of "supercessionism,"[26] among other problems. As we noted earlier, the key problem with the traditional sequence is the fact that it is premised and constructed on a flawed theological notion and a misreading of the Hebrew scriptures that imposes Christian interpretations on selected texts "as if these Hebrew scriptures actually contained a blueprint for the words Jesus spoke and the deeds he did,"[27] regardless of the fact that the rabbis (and the Midrashic tradition) of Judaism interpret these texts differently. Besides arrogance, an evident implication related to this theology is its underlying premise of the divine planning of the story of salvation with such precision that the exact words were placed on the mouths of prophets and the quills of scribes that would be fulfilled centuries later.

We agree with Spong this is too "cosy" and "circular" a theory, and one that turns God into "a master planner in the sky who dictated the content of the prophetic writings so that a divine plan would be seen to occupy vast sweeps of time as one unfolding whole."[28] In our view, such a prescriptive theory of "fulfilment" arrogantly relegates the integrity of the Hebrew scriptures under the dictates of the Christian New Testament and offers a warped view of our sacred texts and how these have evolved. Furthermore it is evident how such a position's arrogance and self-righteousness may have led to anti-Semitic views and practices. In a postcolonial and complex world of cultures and religions it seems to us that the frame of reference that informed the crafting of the Service of Nine Lessons needs to be deconstructed and critically interrogated drawing from recent scholarship in biblical studies, hermeneutics, theology and religious studies. Certainly, in our present context of discourse around cultures and hybrid and hyphenated[29] identities, any revision will need to give greater agency to Jesus' Jewishness.[30]

A Cross-reference: The Easter Vigil

In evaluating the Nine Lessons, it is instructive to cross-reference to other liturgical celebrations, for the tradition of sequential scripture readings at particular times of the Christian calendar is by no means innovative. On the one hand, looking at the readings in the Easter Vigil sequences may be opened up to similar kinds of critiques as those we level at the Nine Lessons; on the other hand, they may suggest some correctives to the hermeneutics of the Nine Lessons.

The primary example of such reading is the Office of Readings which forms part of the Easter Vigil in increasing numbers of traditions.[31] *Times and Seasons* provides a "choice of readings." In all, twenty-two readings from Hebrew scripture are provided, allowing for "different routes through the reading, each following a particular theme or motif."[32] Five themes are identified: baptism, women in salvation, salvation, renewal and freedom – although in each case, "a minimum of three Old Testament readings should be chosen," it is mandated that the story of "crossing the Red Sea" from Exodus 14 is always used, whatever other choice is allowed, and it is "desirable" that the opening reading is Gen. 1:1–2.4a, a creation narrative. Two of the sequences include Genesis 3 – on "the Fall" – as a second reading. At least at Easter it seems, it is undesirable to begin, as the nine Truro lessons do, with a narrative of the Fall. This small step in the direction of encouragement of diverse pathways through the "meta-narrative" of the Bible is surely to be affirmed, although we would want to suggest that it is still too prescriptive and that at least some of the problems we identify with the Christmas Festival of Nine Lessons and Carols also all too easily hound Christians' Bible reading at the Easter Vigil.

However, *Times and Seasons* also suggests that the Easter Vigil may be celebrated in "a variety of styles" and that "the readings could be followed by silence, interactive Bible study, artistic activity, discussion, testimony, drama, intercession, singing or whatever is appropriate to the context."[33] Marking the Easter Candle, "preparations for the Baptismal Liturgy such as filling a baptismal ewer" and "eating and drinking that are related to the readings" are also commended and mention is also made of "choruses" and "spiritual songs."[34] Notably, this kind of creativity is not commended in relation to Christmas sequence of lessons and carols, although we would wish to stretch further the range of creative responses to scripture readings in the Easter Vigil to include some explicitly postcolonial tactics, such as those we introduce below.

We also note that *Times and Seasons* provides alternative collects in relation to each of its suggested scripture readings at the Easter Vigil. These two prayers are quite different in style: one "follows a traditional collect structure and may be introduced by a Christological response" and the prayer itself then "relates the reading to the work of Christ";[35] the other, beginning in the style of certain Jewish prayers (*Berakah* prayers beginning "Blessed are you...") "reflects the theme of the reading without referring directly to the work of Christ."[36] Some of these prayers in the second style are vivid in their imagery; for example, in relation to the mandatory reading of Exodus 14: "Hear the cry of the enslaved and the homeless today and lead us through the turbulent sea of life to our true home in you."[37] In their awareness of the enslaved and homeless, suffering and broken-hearted, and otherwise afflicted, these prayers in some ways echo at least some of the circumstances in which Eric Milner-White beckoned Christmas worshippers in Cambridge to remember, "in [Jesus'] name," others in need. In their restraint from – at least "directly" – mapping Christ onto these or Hebrew "others," they represent what we would regard as a more appropriate form of prayer in the context of reading a sequence of Hebrew scripture; and from a postcolonial optic, the only appropriate form of the two *Common Worship* options.

Singing Lies

The King's College Service of Nine Lessons and Carols consistently begins with the hymn "Once in Royal David's City," although other hymnody varies somewhat, often including material that stretches beyond the imagination of many old-line hymnals, albeit seemingly entirely confined to "classical" western tradition. It is, then, particularly important to scrutinize the famous text of Cecil Frances Alexander with which the service begins. The text is her attempt to unfold the creedal confession "born of the Virgin Mary" and is one in a series of her children's hymns elaborating on the Apostles' Creed. Children figure heavily in the text: while one, Jesus Christ, is central, "Christian children" are encouraged to be "mild, obedient, good as he," and the climax of the carol is a vision of "his children" – presumably good, obedient, mild ones – "crowned/all in White" like stars in heaven.

Evangelical Lutheran Worship is among a number of contemporary hymnals that simply omit the fanciful imaginings of Jesus' "wondrous childhood" of repeatedly mentioned obedience. Its version of the carol shifts from a second stanza ending with holy presence "with the poor and meek and lowly" to the third stanza's opening image of "our eyes at last" seeing him in "the place where he is gone." Interestingly, one of the alterations made to the traditional text by *Evangelical Lutheran Worship* is to recast the last stanza's final image of "waiting around" in heaven, presumably to make beatific imagery more active: "waiting" becomes "gathering." So we read, "there his children gather round, bright like stars, with glory crowned."[38]

A more comprehensive alteration is offered by the United Church of Christ's *New Century Hymnal* in that, as with all its other contents, the carol is revised to erase gendered references, so "his bed" becomes "a bed," "Lord of all" becomes "Head of all," and so on. In this, the alteration of this particular text reflects the hymnal's "bold commit[ment] to a spirit of inclusiveness"[39] and to search for "language to sing about people that excludes no one – words that all people can sing."[40] Where "extensive" revisions are made to inherited hymnody, this is indicated by a note that the text has been "adapted" and the name of one of the various luminaries (the likes of Carl Daw, Ruth Duck, Marty Haugen, Thomas Troeger, and Miriam

Therese Winter) who "assisted in the revision of hymn texts"[41] often appears alongside. Where a more minor revision is made, the text is designated as being "altered." "Once in Royal David's City" falls into the latter category, yet perhaps more adaptation was needed: for despite the adjustment of gendered language, Cecil Francis Alexander's original verses about Jesus' wondrous childhood remain. And although Mary is no longer a "lowly maiden" with "gentle arms," but a "tender mother whose strong arms" make a cradle for her child, the child himself remains not only "little, weak and helpless," as he must, but "our childhood's pattern" of honour and obedience.

What we may see here reflected in the *New Century Hymnal* is the continuing need for a liberation theology for children, whose experiences and concerns are eclipsed even from much feminist theology, let alone the patriarchal inheritance that feminist theology is anxious to contest.[42] Further, from a postcolonial perspective, the link between perceiving the cultures and natives of Africa, India, the Caribbean, and Pacific and Native Americans as "childish" and of a "child-like nature" and not fully evolved and enlightened has been reinforced by such lyrics.

Problems that may attend to other sung texts in traditional performances of the nine lessons and carols ought to include images centred on the occupation of someone else's land, a God who endorses travel to distant places, bringing light to darkened peoples, the depersonalization of Mary as God and the men take over, and the pervasive presence of empire language which can also be represented in the triumphant beats of the music. These problems are compounded by the fact that they echo ones already found in scripture, where, for instance, Gen. 12:1-8 seems to introduce the idea that God endorses movement and a theology of land that can so readily play into the colonial imagination; just as Isaiah prophesies that "people who walked in darkness have seen a great light" (Isa. 9:2-7), a notion disastrously vulnerable to the notion of White European superiority; and Lk. 1:26-28 may be read as depersonalizing Mary by depicting Jesus as son of God, with Mary perhaps an ambiguous image of internalized patriarchy.

Conclusion: Some Beginnings for an Alternative Version

In the final section of this chapter, we suggest just two means of developing alternatives to inherited versions of Nine Lessons and Carols. Our suggestions are illustrative and unfinished, intended to encourage the reader's creative thought and emphatically not to prescribe others' practice.

Our first suggestion is to experiment with interruption as a liturgical strategy. In the context of the Festival of Nine Lessons and Carols, this may mean interrupting neat *sequences* of readings or it may mean interrupting *particular* readings. Certainly, we would wish to interrupt traditional strings of readings such as those which form the Nine Lessons, and we can imagine different ways in which this might be done. On the one hand, scriptural readings which (not least through the Festival of Nine Lessons and Carols itself) have come to be "expected" at Christmastime might be set alongside other, more surprising or awkward, readings from scripture itself. For instance, within a series of more-or-less expected readings, the narrative of the massacre of the innocents might puncture certain kinds of sentimentality about "the Christmas story" by inviting difficult questions about apparent divine initiative which the canonical narrative presents in the most ambiguous terms, and so complicate any uncritical assumptions about the easy sequencing of "salvation history." At least potentially, such contrapuntal readings[43] could leave hearers with questions which present *frisson* with other biblical texts, provoking what in the context of worship is likely to remain unspoken contest to assumed "authorized" narratives.

Still, on its own, this is not enough, so on the other hand, non-scriptural readings might be used to interrupt traditional scriptural readings. This could mean juxtaposing certain biblical narratives with contemporary "parallels" – perhaps setting the story of the flight into Egypt alongside recent and real "Stories of Exile," such as those found in the Refugee Council publications.[44] Or rather than such "paralleling," it could mean a more (deliberately) chaotic juxtaposition of texts which accents the need for urgent attention to contemporary testimony, difficult to hear as it may be. The point of such interruption is quite consciously to "upset" and "puncture"

the order of things in a way which might be paralleled to the determination to "queer" dominant or "normal" order in queer theology
and theory,[45] as well as is reflected in Michael's case for an Anancy
hermeneutics.[46]

Another precedent for this kind of strategy is the understanding of
challenging Holocaust literature as amounting to something like "the
stories of a new bible" which contest the supposed assurances of
the canon which, however "authoritative," experience is emphatically unable to affirm.[47] Furthermore, a very important liturgical
precedent for this strategy is the work Michael Jagessar has done
to craft a eucharistic liturgy in which classical modes of praise are
interrupted. Michael's work has interjected narratives of asylum
seekers into prayer at the table in a properly disturbing way.[48]
And certainly, Michael's concern to facilitate attention to asylum
seekers can to be transposed into the context of biblical "Christmas
narratives." There may be a certain analogy to be drawn between
Michael's work and the way in which the reproaches of some Good
Friday liturgies suggest "an inversion of the holy history we recite and
recall in the Great Thanksgiving at the Lord's table,"[49] and hence an
occasion for lament in Christian liturgy, although the *novum* aspect
of Michael's work is to bring different narratives, moods and sources
into creative, immediate "collision."[50] And in principle, we see no
reason to restrict such interruption to "themes" which already find
some allusions in the Bible. Anything – therefore, everything – about
which Christians might pray is potentially an appropriate topic for
interruption in the liturgy, and might be the focus of urgent and
insistence encouragement to "look where God's love is looking."[51]

Unexpected kinds of music and song may also foster the kind
of interruption we are imaging here. For instance, among its merits
the *New Century Hymnal* includes among its songs for Christmas,
the Genzo Miwa's carol "Hitsuji wa nemureri" (Sheep Fast Asleep)
from Japan, and Angel Sotto and Lois Bello's "Maglakat na Kita sa
Belen" (Let Us Even Now Go to Bethlehem) from the Philippines.
Notwithstanding our cautions about neo-colonial use of "world
church" song, we see it as sometimes being able to shift moods in
helpful ways and in turn puncture an exclusive sense of "tradition."
What is more, we note that some of the kinds of material incorporated in the *New Century Hymnal* are still waiting to be included

among the carols from King's College, for instance. Robert Beckford's *Jesus Dub: Theology, Music and Social Change*[52] could perhaps serve to animate ways of developing this strategy, and one with origins in Caribbean cultures.

Our second suggestion is to find ways to attend to contextual interpretations of any biblical readings used. In this case, biblical readings would be interpreted by diverse voices that are identified as self-consciously located in distinction to the context of the hearers. At least potentially, this could allow hearers to gain some critical dissonance with their own situation, geo-political and otherwise. In developing an alternative to the Festival of Nine Lessons and Carols, a resource such as Walter Dietrich and Ulrich Luz's *The Bible in a World Context*[53] could perhaps be used, rightful criticisms of that work notwithstanding.[54] It includes three theoretical approaches to "contextual hermeneutics" from Latin America (Elsa Tamez), Africa (Justin Ukpong) and Asia (Seiichi Yagi) before offering three contextual readings of Luke chapter 2, a narrative that is naturally prevalent in lectionaries for Christmastime. Excerpts from such perspectives might be used within the liturgical celebration itself as commentaries on the biblical texts, complementing if not contesting the scriptural reading, but perhaps might also – for instance where it is possible to imagine "adult Sunday schools" – be used in educational settings outside the liturgy in preparation for the liturgical celebration. While providing some engagement with contextual interpretations of scriptural texts might immediately seem less confrontational than the just-commended strategy of interruption, we contend that it may nevertheless provide powerful means of relativizing celebrants' perspectives by setting their (spoken or unspoken) assumptions about the meanings of a text alongside possibly very different but related understandings, allowing for the possibility of subtle approaches to well-worn texts.

We wish to make one final observation. We find encouragement in the complex and messy historical development of the liturgical celebration of Christmas, which is inseparably bound up with particular cultural circumstances in the early Christian milieu. The exact origins of the identification of 25 December as the birthday of Jesus are fascinating, but vague. In brief, there are two main theories, one which relates to contemporaneous pagan celebration of the

Festival of the Unconquered Sun, and the other that represents a creative development of widespread Jewish midrash.[55]

In pointing to these theories, what we wish to assert is the important precedent of concern with engagement in diverse cultural contexts. However, we are of course well aware that neither of these theories is free from imperializing tendencies, and so it is crucial that we offer some significant qualification. Both of these theories are intentionally confrontational in asserting the primacy of Jesus over other objects of religious devotion and honour. We would not wish to commend this, and want instead to assert the vital importance of more modest, humble and dialogical means of relating to others' values and religious ideals – and to do so by more truthful, if not less creative, means. Indeed, we would commend practices of relating to others that might self-consciously regard themselves as not simply as alternatives, but as *correctives*, to the arrogant tactics that underlie these Christmas theories. At the very least, that is to say that the Festival of Nine Lessons and Carols finds its own context in a larger tradition, the whole of which stands in need of considerable correction, and which points to a much larger project of which this chapter may represent a start.

6 Images of Baptism and Ministry

Introducing the Conversation

We are both ordained ministers, and as such we are cognizant of the need to interrogate practices, rites and images of Christian ministry within the ecclesial traditions with which we are most familiar. Our intention in this chapter is to start a conversation around the theological and biblical interpretations that shape the practices, rites and images of Christian ministry, and the ways these have evolved. We explore through specific examples of our contemporary contexts whether "updated" and revised practices, rites and images might actually re-inscribe imperial language and agenda. In this, we offer a very particular trajectory into the significant concern of this whole project to "uncover" the theology that informs the crafting and practice of liturgies. From a postcolonial perspective we wish to encourage critical conversation about how liturgies broadly concerned with ministry engage individualism, communal identity, servanthood and assumptions about belonging in the context of colonial history.

David Joy, writing in the context of India and with specific reference to images of ministry, notes that "the imperial presence in the advancing and interpreting of texts related to images of ministry cannot be overlooked."[1] This holds true for all the rites and practices of the Christian church located by both the colonized and the colonizers. These rites cannot be read outside of the context of historical realities, past and present. Drawing on the works of postcolonial voices such as R. S. Sugirtharajah, Musa Dube and Kwok Pui-lan, we can rephrase some of the questions they have raised in the context of biblical hermeneutics and theology to help with our interrogation of rites, practices and theology related to baptism, ordination and images of ministry. For instance: What in these rites and practices encourages colonial hegemony, for instance, by appealing to tradition (e.g. apostolic succession) and centralizing authority[2] to marginalize an inclusive ministry, restrict an open table and attempts to speak for all? Who or what tradition is the reference point for authenticity and originality? How are these rites, passages and images bound or restricted by this and then re-inscribed in what is supposed to be modern liturgies and practices? What about the notion of God's elected people, the chosen and set-apart ones, and how is this reflected in the rites of baptism and ordination and images of ministry? With scholars such as Barbara Brown Taylor we wish to question emphasis on the notion of "setting apart" that pervades these rites, especially as it is also at the heart of imperial proclivities with a penchant for advancing binaries through games of insider/outsider, civilized/primitive, savage/noble and children of light versus those from those of darkness. Barbara Brown Taylor's own particular perspective on the difficulties of being set apart is not itself postcolonial, though it does offer an evocative narrative of identification with others strongly resistant to binaries. In her "memoir of faith," *Leaving Church*, she recounts her gradual movement away from parish ministry into other forms of work and identity. One luminous passage focuses on an incident in her last weeks in the parish, at a gathering at the home of a parishioner:

> After my supper had settled I wandered down to the pool, where I watched swimming children splitting beams of underwater light with their bodies. I had baptized many of them, and I loved seeing them all shrieking and paddling around together in that one big pool. Suddenly to my right there was a deeper yell, the sound of scrambling feet on cement, and then a large plop as a fully clothed adult landed in the water.
> I stood back and watched the mayhem that ensued. All around me, people were grabbing people and wrestling them toward the water. The dark night air was full of pool spray and laughter. The kids were going crazy. Several people hunting for potential victims turned toward me, their faces lit with smiles. When they saw who I was they turned away again…

Eventually, however, she finds herself hurled into the water…

> [W]hen I broke the surface, I looked around at all those shining people with makeup running down their cheeks, with hair plastered to their

heads, and I was so happy to be one of them. If being ordained meant being set apart from them, then I did not want to be ordained anymore. I wanted to be human.

Brown adds that "in that healing pool with all those other flawed beings of light, I looked around and saw them as I had never seen them before, while some of them looked at me the same way."[3] Her story powerfully relates dynamics of power that attach to Christian ministry, as well as her own yearning to be rid of a strongly felt binary between lay and ordained. Interestingly, this yearning is manifest for Brown in a quasi-baptismal scenario.

According to R. S. Sugirtharajah, polarizing ways of imagining our world in terms of binaries are "a valuable ally in maintaining imperial ideology and reinforcing power relations between the ruler and the ruled."[4] Images from the Christian tradition, such as Saviour of the World, Light to the Nations and Light from Light, combine to project an imperial Christ, and there are many more examples. We add our voices to Elisabeth Schüssler-Fiorenza's plea for fresh images that do not re-inscribe *kyriocentric* language of empire,[5] and in what follows explore ways in which binaries are maintained in certain sacramental practices.

Baptism and Ministry

We begin with baptism as this is a central rite in Christian worship, widely shared across a wide range of ecclesial traditions. Although the form of the rite differs in mode (immersion in water, pouring of water, and so on) and ceremonial simplicity or richness (whether or not additional ancillary rites of signing with the cross, anointing with oil, or the giving and reception of a candle are involved), Christian baptism occurs as Trinitarian identification of God is made in relation to a person brought into contact with water. A commonly acknowledged characteristic of the rite, whatever the particular ecclesial setting, is that "it shapes our primary and continuing identity as Christians."[6] The well-known and widely-lauded World Council of Churches document *Baptism, Eucharist and Ministry* states the following about baptism:

Baptism is the sign of new life through Jesus Christ. It unites the one baptized with Christ and with his people. The New Testament scriptures and the liturgy of the Church unfold the meaning of baptism in various images which express the riches of Christ and the gifts of his salvation. These images are sometimes linked with the symbolic uses of water in the Old Testament. Baptism is participation in Christ's death and resurrection (Rom. 6:3–5; Col. 2:12); a washing away of sin (I Cor. 6:11); a new birth (John 3:5); an enlightenment by Christ (Eph. 5:14); a re-clothing in Christ (Gal. 3:27); a renewal by the Spirit (Titus 3:5); the experience of salvation from the flood (I Peter 3:20–21); an exodus from bondage (I Cor. 10:1–2) and a liberation into a new humanity in which barriers of division whether of sex or race or social status are transcended (Gal. 3:27–28; I Cor. 12:13). The images are many but the reality is one.[7]

While the document has more to say about baptism, one is struck by some of the traits of colonial discourse that may be deduced from this core extract: discontinuity from former life, rejection of diversity through a normative oneness, and preference towards a set-apart group that may well find expression in the restricting of hospitality.

Let us further explore some of these notions by focusing on the "affirmation of commitment" associated with baptism and found in numerous places in the Church of England's *Common Worship* range of resources, apart from many other ritual books around the world.[8] This affirmation makes an interesting place to concentrate reflection on baptism and ministry from a postcolonial perspective. This affirmation reads:

Will you continue in the apostles' teaching and fellowship,
in the breaking of bread, and in the prayers?
With the help of God, I will.

Will you persevere in resisting evil,
and, whenever you fall **into** sin, repent and return to the Lord?
With the help of God, I will.

Will you proclaim by word and example
the good news of God in Christ?
With the help of God, I will.

Will you seek and serve Christ in all people,
loving your neighbour as yourself?
With the help of God, I will.

> Will you acknowledge Christ's authority over human society,
> by prayer for the world and its leaders,
> by defending the weak, and by seeking peace and justice?
> **With the help of God, I will.**[9]

These words are part of the baptism service in the *Common Worship* volume *Christian Initiation*, and they may be addressed at baptism to persons able to answer for themselves. They are also used at confirmation. Furthermore, the words are part of a service of congregational re-affirmation of baptism, the rubrics of which recommend for use only infrequently – once or twice a year. But they also re-appear in the book of *Daily Prayer* and elsewhere in the context of a "thanksgiving for the mission of the church," and in that context may be used more often, as indeed is the case in the main volume of *Common Worship* where it is suggested that the affirmation of commitment may be appended to creedal statements and affirmations of faith, and so in that way used on any occasion. In any event, use of the affirmation of commitment is no doubt intended to allow for an affirmation of particular *practices* that are understood to be complementary to Christian *belief*, which juxtaposition of this text to a creed may well accentuate.

The text of the affirmation is itself adapted from other recent Anglican resources. Commentaries on the *Common Worship* material ascribe the text to the Anglican Church of Canada's 1985 *Book of Alternative Services*.[10] The Canadian text, however, has a slightly longer history in that it earlier appeared in the Episcopal Church in the USA's *Book of Common Prayer* of 1979. Leonel Mitchell's commentary on the ECUSA book refers to work of the drafting committee for the text as if it were written for the US book.[11] In any case, what the *Common Worship* commentaries do not note is that the *Common Worship* text is itself an adaptation of the North American text (of whatever precise provenance), and that the amendment has a somewhat different tone to the earlier version. Mitchell refers to the latter two questions in the affirmation suggesting the "social implications of the gospel" which the baptized embrace in their participation in the sacrament. However, the final question to which he refers, and which it seems the American committee drafted, reads:

Will you strive for justice and peace and among all people, and respect the dignity of every human being?

This earlier text was, then, changed in *Common Worship*, and we would suggest that the change was to make the social impli-cations of the gospel somewhat gentler and more passive than in this earlier version. The softening or dumbing down is conveyed in the choice of verbs: from "striving" and "respecting," the key words shift to "acknowledging," "praying," "defending," and "seeking." Furthermore, the "all" and "every" of the earlier text are amended to distinguish "leaders" from others, and to underscore a sense of Christ's "authority over" society, which so closely juxtaposed with reference to "leaders" may too easily invite the sense of Christ's authority being mediated in a hierarchical manner.

The changes made in *Common Worship* to this baptismal affirmation introduce at least some of the issues with which this chapter is concerned. They suggest colonial intentions through: notions of authority, "holy order," the "ordering" of persons, and how sacraments – especially baptism and holy orders – might relate to a wider sense of divine mediation to and/or through persons. We wish to make a modest contribution to an ongoing conversation about how sacramentality might be conceived in relation to postco-lonial convictions; and we wish to do so through careful scrutiny of specific texts, actions and practices that shape liturgical celebration.

The *Common Worship* affirmation of commitment suggests a notion of holy order that is bound up in Christ's authority over society and the mediation of divine order through human leadership. We affirm that human persons may depict and manifest divine presence to one another; what concerns us about the *Common Worship* script we have cited is what we regard as the naïvety of its alliances between divine and human authority. Or perhaps this is more intentional than naïve. For colonial history is replete with examples of how theology was (and is being) used to justify the domination of smaller and weaker peoples on the very premise that the colonizing power received its authority from divine sources. We suggest that the baptismal affirmation needs to be better "traditioned" in things that can readily be learned by almost the least attention to "church history" – in awareness of the subjugation that has resulted from the assumption that the ordering of societies reflects divine authority, or that active and enervating "striving" may not be necessary to scrutinize and enlarge the capacities of human communities to mediate divine love for the world.

It may be that the *Common Worship* amendment to the earlier version of the baptismal text is an attempt to echo certain biblical material, such as Romans 13:1-7 or 1 Peter 2:13-17. Yet, these texts are also not value free as they are ideologically conditioned, and their use in the affirmation smacks of ambivalence. We suggest that it does not nuance as it needs to its appropriation of the notions such texts present. At the very least, resonance with such scriptural texts in the scripts of the liturgy needs to be subject to something akin to the lectionary dynamic of asserting that the gospel is an interpretive lens for the rest of the canon, so that the authority and practical import of wider biblical material is negotiated in terms of a christological (not kyriological) centre in which the person and practice of Jesus become optics for reading the rest of the Bible. The memory of Jesus' words about "giving to Caesar what is Caesar's" (Mark 12:17) is of course only one part of what can be discerned about Jesus' attitude and action in relation to authority, leadership, the necessary "defence" of the weak by also giving them a chance to cut loose their denied tongue, prayerful action (pointedly in the scriptural memory, whatever the historicity, of his juxtaposition of his discourse about prayer in the context of the action of overturning tables in the temple), and teaching about justice and peace.

We suggest that a postcolonial perspective on baptism and ministry cannot be built on the *Common Worship* amendment to the earlier baptismal affirmation. Without specific attention to particular contexts, abstract talk of "Christ's authority over human society" is at best sanguine, to put it mildly. Moreover, ritualized in ceremonial scenes like the *Common Worship* affirmation, it is irresponsible, and needs to be confronted by *anamnesis,* and not least memories of suffering that can be learned from other parts of the liturgical repertoire. A postcolonial perspective on baptism and ministry can only and insistently be built on the affirmation of "the dignity of every human being" – at least if baptism (or orders) is indeed to serve as a "sacrament of a new society" (in Rowan Williams's stylish rhetoric[12]). It is therefore to our minds a matter of regret that *Common Worship* amended a text with a widening use (not least ecumenically) to move it in a most unfortunate direction.

Ordination and Images of Ministry

Let us reiterate here that our agenda is to interrogate and expose imperial impulses that may be linked to liturgical rites of the Christian tradition. Hence, in this section on ordination and images of ministry, we want to especially look for ways in which the rite(s) and images may project an imperial Christ and church, whether diversity is allowed free play, how tradition is employed (is it deployed to justify authority, for instance?) and whether the liturgies of ordination from the two ecclesial traditions under scrutiny restrict hospitality. Two particular images that will be of interest to us are those of shepherd and servant, both of which raise interesting questions given their possible link to docility, following and subjugation. To what extent do these two images actually signify and subvert?

Baptism and Ordination: The Connections

If our reflections on baptism concentrated on a particular text – the *Common Worship* "affirmation of commitment" – our consideration of ordination rites takes a wider view, looking at texts, symbols, rubrics and ceremonial dimensions of liturgy. In particular, our present consideration draws on the practice of ordination in the Church of England and the Uniting Church in Australia (and therefore on our own geographical locations as well as our own Anglican and Reformed ecclesial traditions). In its context following a previous section on baptism, it is also important to note that part of the wider view taken here requires an appreciation of the ways in which contemporary ordination rites are themselves intentionally related to baptismal rites. Hence, our search for a wider view is related to what we have articulated about baptism in the earlier section of this chapter.

A connection between baptism and ordination is made in various ways in liturgies, sometimes explicitly, as in the introduction spoken by the bishop in the *Common Worship* ordination services: "in baptism the whole church is summoned to witness to God's love and to work for the coming of his kingdom." This is a major plank of the theological framework in which ordained ministries, among "a variety of ministries" in the "royal priesthood" of God, are set. This understanding is sustained throughout the liturgy, echoed in declarations, questions and prayer-texts, such that this opening conviction is patterned, as it were, throughout the whole service. Indeed, the thoroughgoingness of this feature of the rites must count as one of their key achievements and a point on which they must be acclaimed. Within contemporary Anglican thinking, this framing of ordination in terms of baptism is much indebted to the "baptismal ecclesiology" associated with Louis Weil and others, although the point remains that baptismal practice across Anglicanism in different provinces of the Anglican Communion remains quite divergent, and that particular Anglican churches (nationally/regionally, as well no doubt at congregational level) have competing understandings of the sacrament (not least the ECUSA, which appears to be in retreat from some of the more progressive aspects of its baptismal theology).

Framing understanding of ordination in the context of baptism is itself a theological move that found important impetus in the Second Vatican Council, although the Roman Catholic tradition resolutely distinguishes between "ministerial" and other priesthood in ways that are more blurred in other traditions (some more than others). The Uniting Church in Australia also grounds its understandings of ordination in a baptismal context, though the ordination services themselves lack the direct reference to baptism which is emphasized in the Church of England's rites. Baptism is mentioned in the liturgy of ordination in the vows, when ordinands are asked the question

> "Do you receive baptism and the eucharist, instituted by our Lord as signs and seals of his gospel; and do you resolve to celebrate these sacraments with the people of God?"

"Sacraments" are again mentioned in the presentation of the Bible, with the given Bible said to be a sign of "authority given to you." An intended connection between baptism and ordination is, however, made plainly apparent in the recent "Brief Statement on Ordination" by the Uniting Church in Australia (UCA), a document for which the chair of the church's Working Group on Worship, Paul Walton was the principal author, and which begins with the heading "Baptism: the foundation of all Christian ministry." Stressing that baptism is a sign of renewal of an individual life in Christ, but also the incorporation of that life into the Christian community, "the body of Christ," it then draws attention to the statement in the baptism service that "claimed by God we are given the gift of the Holy Spirit that we may live as witnesses to Jesus Christ, share his ministry…" Although baptism is not named in this sequence of theological ideas, the baptismal context in which they are spoken secures the sense that this "claiming" and "giving" which lead to coming to share in Christ's ministry is associated with baptism. The Basis of Union, on which the Uniting Church is founded, is also appealed to, which also emphasizes "every member" ministry (para. 13, where the phrase is used), although baptism is not there named as the foundation for such ministry. It seems that the Uniting Church has latterly moved in the direction of seeking to articulate a baptismal ecclesiology.

Although English Anglican and Australian Uniting ordination rites share to some extent a baptismal underpinning, there are significant differences between the two, beginning with the fact they ordain to different, although related, ministries. The Church of England, as Anglicans elsewhere, has a "threefold ministry" of bishops, priests and deacons. The Uniting Church ordains deacons and ministers of the Word, "which are distinct, [but] also overlap." The overlapping is intentionally borne out in the liturgy, where the same texts are used, although the ordinand's vows are in a different order to the order for deacons and the order for ministers of the Word, reflecting perhaps different priorities in responsibilities common to both. Anglicans also call their priests "presbyters," a term also used by the Uniting for their ministers of the Word. "Presbyter" remains the ancillary term in both traditions, although this has been contested by persons in each tradition. Uniting ordinations are always "an act of presbytery," while Anglican ordinations are always "presided over" (ordination of a bishop), and specific liturgical roles are defined for deacons in ordination services, whereas they are not in other services. These differences and similarities point to some of the most obvious ways in which comparing Anglican and Uniting orders of ordination is not a comparison of like with like.

Comments on the Anglican Rites

The role of the bishop (who must at present be male) in English Anglican ordinations is an obvious focus of a nexus of concern with "authority," such that when a bishop is himself ordained (and consecrated – the only one of the three ministries to which this additional term is applied, and with a possible corresponding ritual of anointing, discussed below), there is special attention to both "authority for ordination" and a "royal mandate" for it to take place. This amplifies the current running throughout the other two ministries with oaths made at "the declaration of assent," that is of allegiance to the sovereign, of canonical obedience to the bishop, and the declaration that "in public prayer and administration of the sacraments, I will use only the forms of service which are authorized or allowed by Canon" – hence, concern with authority to present and preside at particular liturgies itself becomes a matter subject to authority. Although this declaration is not itself read in ordinations of deacons and priests, as it is at the ordination of a bishop, the preface of the declaration is always to be printed within any order of service. Across the threefold ministry "authority" to minister is associated with the Bible.

Both priests and bishops are associated with the traditional "pastoral" role of the shepherd, and the liturgy of ordination for priests uses images associated with shepherding – watching, searching, guiding – as a key cluster matched only by another concerned with calling, telling, proclaiming. A bishop to be consecrated is exhorted, "With a shepherd's love, they are to be merciful, but with firmness; to minister discipline, but with compassion." A prayer for the bishop asks that "he may use his authority to heal, not to hurt; to build up, not to destroy," and a question to the bishop, itself framed in terms of "discipline," asks if he will exercise "authority with justice, courtesy and love," while another question requires him to affirm that he will "refute error" and "hand on entire the faith that is entrusted" to him. This is echoed in a more diminutive form in declarations required of priests, when faithful ministry of "doctrine and sacraments of Christ as the Church of England has received them" is mentioned, "so that the people committed to your charge may be defended against error and flourish in the faith." Deacons are asked if they will "accept the discipline of this Church" and priests if they will "accept and minister the discipline of this Church" and both are asked if they will "respect authority duly exercised within it." Deference to the authority of bishops is signalled in the term of address employed when candidates for the priesthood and diaconate are presented for ordination: "Reverend Father."

There is an apparent, and at times very obvious, sense of gradation in the threefold ministry in Anglican orders, with a hierarchy of authority leading to the bishop, even as a number of tasks are shared between bishops, priests and deacons, others between bishops and priests, and others between bishops acting together. The gradation can be illustrated by reference to how the notion of "justice" is related to order within the threefold ministry, such that deacons are to have "a life of visible self-giving" and "bring the needs of the world before the Church in intercession" (the latter being a somewhat weaker echo of the Episcopal Church in the USA's description of the deacon's work as "to interpret to the Church the needs, concerns and hopes of the world") as they work to "search out the poor and weak, the sick and the lonely and those who are oppressed and powerless, reaching out into the forgotten corners of the world, that the love of God may be made visible." The word justice is not explicitly mentioned, but the sense of searching out the vulnerable is weaker than the task given to priests, who are to "resist evil, support the weak, defend the poor, and intercede for all in need." In turn, the sense of this resistance to evil is weaker than the task given to bishops, who are "to confront injustice" ("following the example of the prophets"), presumably in their representative capacity. It should be noted, however, that descriptions of the bishops' role at times fold into close relationship with the activities with which deacons are to be concerned: bishops are to "have a special care for the poor, the outcast and those who are in need." This statement is followed immediately by another more akin to the Church of England's liturgy's view of priests' work: "to seek out those who are lost and lead them home rejoicing, declaring the absolution and forgiveness of sins to those who turn to Christ." This no doubt intentionally reflects the fact that a bishop will have been previously ordained both deacon and priest, so that his ministry as a bishop is incremental, as it were, on these previous experiences, charges and callings.

The laying on of hands in each of the orders also differs across the threefold ministry, and is enveloped by concerns for authority. For deacons, "the bishop alone lays his hands on the heads of those ordained." For priests, other "priests share with the bishop in laying hands on the heads of those ordained to the presbyterate. They do so at the invitation of the bishop." For bishops, "at least two bishops must join the Archbishop of the Province or his deputy in the act of ordination." Although theologically central to the act of ordination, the laying on of hands is not the only gesture which mediates meaning in the service, and other gestures are congruent with the hierarchy expressed in the laying on of hands.

While the ordination service for deacons, unlike that for priests, specifically mentions that "as [Christ] washed the feet of his disciples, so they must wash the feet of others," a rubric allows for the bishop to wash the feet of newly ordained deacons before the reading of the gospel text remembering Jesus' washing of disciples' feet. The parallel rubric in the ordination service for priests allows the bishop to "anoint the palms" of newly ordained priests, with the accompanying words: "May God, who anointed the Christ with the Holy Spirit at his baptism, anoint and empower you to reconcile and bless his people." At the ordination of bishops, an archbishop may anoint the newly ordained bishop on the head, with these words:

> May God, who anointed the Christ with the Holy Spirit at his baptism, anoint and empower you to bring good news to the poor, to proclaim release to the captives, to set free those who are oppressed and to proclaim the acceptable year of the Lord.

In the ceremonial of the services for ordaining priests and bishops, we see a gradation culminating in the bishop. The words addressed to the bishop are also relevant to how the bishop's role is supposed to be related to justice. He is here charged to "set free those who are oppressed" – with this line and the other components in the anointing charge suggesting an astonishingly literal association with Christ. Not only are Christ and anointing juxtaposed in the second line of the charge, but this happens in a direct re-iteration of what is sometimes referred to as "Jesus' first sermon" – his reading from the scroll of Isaiah as remembered in Luke 4.

In its lack of nuance, the association of the bishop and Christ in this ceremonial scene throws stark light on preoccupation with "authority," as discussed above. Christic images are also themselves intensified across the orders for the threefold ministry: deacons are reminded that they are to share the ministry of Christ, "who for our sake took the form of a servant." They are to remember that the people among whom they minister "are made in God's image and likeness." In the parallel part of the order for priests, the people are described as "treasure," "Christ's own flock, bought by the shedding of [Christ's] blood on the cross." In the parallel part of the order for bishops, the people are described as Christ's "flock," as they are in relation to priests, but also as Christ's "beloved bride." The move across the threefold ministry from God's image to Christ's bride maps images of intimacy onto the hierarchy of authority.

Comments on the Uniting Rites

The Uniting Church in Australia has two orders for ordination, one for deacons and the other for ministers of the Word. Persons in these orders are ordained once, to one or the other ministry, which is to say that the diaconate is not a step on the way to progressing to presbyteral ministry. The Uniting Church has shifted in its terms for presbyteral ministry, sometimes favouring the term "presbyter" but opting for "Minister of the Word" in its current documents and liturgical rites. Whereas the Anglican rites are inscribed with gradients, the two Uniting Church orders are intentionally "clearly similar." Indeed, the rubrics and the scripture readings indicated for the two services are identical. With the exception of references to either "deacon" or "minister of the Word," the texts of the ordination services themselves are much the same.

The similarities of the two rites are no doubt intended to quash any notion of "creeping superiority" by those ordained to one vocation over those ordained to the other. Resistance to any suggestion that presbyteral ministry is in any sense superior to diaconal ministry has been an abiding mark of Uniting Church debate about ordination, which has at times been fierce and which has been sustained with some intensity throughout the relatively short period since the

Uniting Church was inaugurated in 1977. In just thirty years, the Uniting Church has oscillated in its understandings of ordination, as is made clear by perusal of the recent collection of theological documents from the UCA edited by Rob Bos and Geoff Thompson, *Theology for Pilgrims*.[13] Thompson and Bos's documentary trail through Uniting Church history reveals how later synods declared earlier theologies of ordination, elaborated at earlier synods, to be "faulty."[14] Their collection especially represents the way in which a 1991 report "Ministry in the Uniting Church" was very strongly contested by a 1994 report "Ordination and Ministry in the Uniting Church." The latter report's pre-fix "ordination and..." no doubt intentionally points to where adequate reflection was considered to be missing in the report at fault. The latter report was much more closely developed in conscious relation to ecumenical understanding of ordination, while the earlier one stresses aspects of Australian contexts which the report supposed to call for distinctive patterns of ministry in the Uniting Church. Weighting towards Australian contexts and a perhaps tenuous connection to the tradition meant that the report was later seen as ecumenically insensitive and idiosyncratic at best. While it may now be that a trajectory is beginning to settle in the UCA's thinking about ordination (at least in the UCA's official understandings if not in more popular consciousness), the Basis of Union, in its acknowledgement that the UCA came into being "in a period of reconsideration of traditional forms of the ministry"[15] seems to have made a hostage to fortune which has enabled the views represented in the 1991 report to remain commonplace in the understanding of Uniting Church members, including its ordained ministers. Within the Uniting Church's oscillating official positions, and the diversity of thought concerning ordination among its members, it might be said that to some extent the earlier report can be regarded as the one which leans towards postcolonial insights (though they are not articulated as such in the report itself). Yet the very public disagreement and dissent about ordination in the Uniting Church invites consideration as to how postcolonial convictions are engaged with the Christian tradition,[16] so as to problematize it, rather than simply circuiting its claims, as arguably the 1991 report did.[17]

Against this controversial background to ordination in the Uniting Church, it becomes apparent why some features of its ordination liturgies are as they are. The likeness of the rite for ordination for deacons and that for ordination of ministers of the Word includes their same use of an artful ordination prayer with a threefold structure which invokes the divine as "holy God," "merciful God," "faithful God" and which contains a number of striking juxtapositions, such as when God is praised as "beyond human sight, above human thought, infinite and unsearchable," before beckoning the Holy Spirit "gentle as a dove, burning as fire." Indeed, the texts of the services for deacons and ministers of the Word are identical, except only that the vows made by ordinands are presented in a different order. Both are asked first if they "confess anew" Christ as "Lord." Secondly, both are then asked about their belief that they are "truly called" to the "office and work" to which they are to be ordained. Thirdly, both are then asked that they "receive the witness to Christ in the holy Scriptures" and about their intention "to undertake to proclaim from these the gospel of Jesus Christ in word and deed." At this point, the questions diverge: deacons are asked if they will announce good news "to those outside the community of faith, stand alongside those who suffer, and work for justice and peace." Two questions come prior to this one for ministers of the Word, and concern the minister of the Word's reception of the sacraments – a parallel to the prior question immediately preceding it about receiving the scriptures – and then about their "endeavour to be a faithful pastor of God's people," equipping their ministry and mission, and working with them to build up the body of Christ. Sacramental imagery is therefore frontloaded in the arrangement of the questions to ministers of the Word. Only then does the question relating to "those outside the community of faith" appear, such that the emphasis falls most emphatically on the gathered congregation as a centre for the minister of the Word's attention. After the question to deacons about those outside the community of faith, the questions about sacraments and endeavour to be a faithful pastor appear, although in opposite order to ministers of the Word, that is, faithful pastor before reception of the sacraments.

At this point, the arrangements of the questions again converge, as both are asked about diligent Bible study and disciplined and holy living, acceptance of historic creeds "of the holy catholic Church" and intention to use them in worship (a parallel to resolve to celebrate sacraments), embrace of "the faith and unity of the holy catholic and apostolic Church as described in the Basis of Union," the reference to the founding document here juxtaposed to foundational creeds of the Church catholic. Just as it is the second of two to invoke the catholicity of the Church (with the Uniting Church's place within the catholic Church emphasized in other parts of the liturgy), this question is the first of two to make explicit mention of the Basis of Union. The following question therefore asks if the minister is willing to be "guided" by the Basis of Union and to "submit yourself" to the Church's discipline. The juxtaposition of the words "submit" and "yourself" are no doubt intended to evoke the sense that such submission is voluntary, freely volitional. The next question then asks that "learning from" confessional documents of the UCA, the minister will then "diligently teach" (no doubt a conscious parallel in relation to particular denominational resources, that they "diligently study" the Bible), particularly to uphold the "centrality of the person and work of Jesus Christ and the grace which justifies … through faith." Here the latter part of the question remembers a reformed stress, while its reference to Christ is an echo of a particular emphasis often suggested to be especially distinctive of the Basis of Union.[18] Without using the word "catholic," a final question zooms out again to concern "peace and unity among all Christian people," again negotiating the local and universal foci of earlier questions.

Unlike Anglican priests, ministers of the Word in the Uniting Church will not previously have been ordained deacon. This is a clear difference between the two traditions. The Uniting orders are at pains to emphasize that it perceives its practice to be enacted "within the one holy catholic and apostolic Church," as are documents of the Uniting Church on ordination to resist the sense of hierarchy between the two ministries, with ministers of the Word perceived to be higher or in more advanced positions than deacons. Indeed, by opting to employ the same texts in each service – albeit with some slight variation in arrangement of the vows – the orders emphatically impress this conviction. And, unlike the Anglican tradition, the Uniting Church does not have bishops, but understands the act of ordination to belong to the presbytery, a collective body where episcope is exercised communally although the notion of episcope is not invoked in the Uniting ordination services.

Other distinctive features of the UCA orders in comparison to the English Anglican ones include the greater stress on personalization in the former, such that "a narration of steps" about the ordinand is an integral part of the UCA liturgy: a "charge" is personalized to the particular minister (although rubrics stress that the charge is intended as opportunity to "remind the ordinand of the dignity and importance of the office" they are embracing and to "exhort as to the seriousness of the ministry to be entered"). Furthermore, the ordinand makes a personal "statement" as part of the service in which they state their faith and affirm their calling to ministry. Each of these features is lacking in the Anglican orders considered above, which place a greater emphasis on the order to be entered and limit the candidate's capacity at least to articulate how they may personally interpret the experiences which have led them to seek ordination or their experience of the act of ordination itself. Although the Uniting Church charge is clearly intended to have a certain kind of gravity – the rubrics clustering language of dignity, exhortation and seriousness – there is a sense of modesty, or understatement, or restraint from grandiosity as compared with the Anglican rites: they elide expressions in the Anglican orders about "weight" and "earnest," such as in statements like "you cannot bear the weight of this calling in your own strength...," "pray earnestly..."

If language differs between the Anglican and Uniting rites, key ceremonial also diverges. As opposed to the particular restriction of the gesture of laying on of hands to the bishop in the case of deacons, bishop and priests in the case of priests, and bishops in the case of bishops, in both ordination services of the Uniting Church, "the presbytery appoints those of its members who are to take part" (rubric 12). It is not that concern for order is abandoned, and issues of authority are clearly being negotiated in this statement – for instance, the appointment of persons to lay on hands is seemingly not the ordinand's decision, although in practice the ordinand may perhaps be consulted as one belonging to the presbytery. Furthermore, "in special circumstances" members of other presbyteries "may be associated with the ordaining presbytery in order to participate" in the laying on of hands. This suggests that the involvement of other presbyteries is understood to be exceptional rather than normal, and moreover, insists that the authority to ordain belongs to a particular presbytery even when others are "associated." Such association is clearly ancillary. More notable than each of these particular features is, however, that the ordaining presbytery, in appointing persons to lay hands upon the ordinand in the act of ordination, "shall [appoint] at least two ordained ministers and two lay persons." This inclusion of laypersons in the core gesture involved in ordination is a clear divergence from the various practices in the rites of the Church of England, which in their differences nevertheless are restricted to other clergypersons, apart from each centring on the bishop. Despite the Anglican orders emphasizing in their texts a baptismal ecclesiology which invites a repeated stress on the call to ministry extended to the whole church, albeit responded to and expressed in different ways, the Uniting Church gesture of sharing this central action among lay and ordained persons may most effectively suggest a deep baptismal ecclesiology. Here, gesture may "speak a thousand words." However, given the controversies about ordination in the Uniting Church, it perhaps remains to be seen whether ordained ministry will itself collapse under the weight of what we called the Basis of Union's hostage to fortune, recognizing changing patterns of ministry. In the Uniting Church, ordination rites face revision under pressures that wish to dismantle ordained ministry, rather than any widespread desire to reconfigure it for postcolonial "reasons."

Postcolonial Questions on Rites as Practised in Both Ecclesial Traditions

The relationship between church and empire is a complex one and liturgical practices and rites associated with these practices lie at the heart of this complexity. This is one of our fundamental points throughout the work. If it is impossible to understand Christianity outside of empire, then liturgical practices stand in need of inter-rogation as these are the heart of Christian practices. As Joerg Rieger writes: "[w]ithout understanding how we are shaped by Empire all the way into our deepest desires, we cannot properly identify the theological surplus, those intuitions and insights that point us beyond the horizons of empire."[19]

The foregoing and necessarily brief introductory sections on Anglican and Uniting Church of Australia rites related to ordination and images of ministry raise a number of questions when viewed through postcolonial optics. Significantly, juxtaposing the rites of two differing ecclesial traditions brings to the fore the possibility of an engaging conversation which is already in play because of the historical development of the two ecclesial traditions. For while these rites are similar and different in terms of intention, it is evident that in the case of the UCA, located in a former colony, these have been crafted by an ecclesial ethos that gives more agency to the participation of laity (including the symbolic act of laying on of hands), to an emphasis on the gathered congregation, and to a greater focus on the stories of the ordinand leading up to the rite, and to an immediacy of the young history of the UCA while linking to the larger history of the Protestant tradition and the Church. In the UCA there is clearly less emphasis on gradation and more of a sense of equality of ministries for its twofold orders.

The differences and similarities outlined in the previous sections raise a number of questions for our postcolonial quest. These questions are all related to the ways authority is understood, used, interpreted and positioned throughout the rite of ordination and its relationship to the images of shepherd and servant *vis à vis* the threefold (or twofold in the case of UCA) and hierarchical proclivities of bishop, presbyter and deacon. To begin with there is the need to scrutinize the claim to authority to minister as one grounded on scriptures by both traditions. As traditions located within Protestant frameworks, scripture is central to an understanding and practice of authority, while still appealing to the past. Though not acknowledged, at play are particular kinds of hermeneutic and readings of the Bible associated with the two ecclesial traditions, mostly similar (but not the same). Scriptures, of course, do not interpret themselves.

Certainly a postcolonial optic will wish to expose any link between where power is located, among whom it is invested and whether there is an agenda to keep it located there. It is this latter tendency in particular which helps to perpetuate exclusionary tactics. Thus one may wish to query, mindful that it is here where authority is invested with legitimacy, whether canonical scriptures are "the sole conveyors of truth."[20] Sugirtharajah rightly issues us with a caveat by observing:

"It is important to establish that the early Christian community was not unified but composed of a whole spectrum of different and rival schools of thought." Hence, a critical question is whether the motivation in terms of both Anglican and UCA rites allow space to "reflect this unsettled character of the early church and question the motives which reject the alternative forms."[21] In other words, how much of the authority of the three- or twofold ministry is an attempt to operate within a normativity that is highly suspicious of divergent voices. Authority may be associated with biblical sources, yet the way we have arrived at the canon of scriptures raises question about the biblical agenda. And the way these have been read to influence the rites of ordination will not be ideologically free or neutral. The challenge before us is how to engage with the voices of our past traditions as "living interlocutors from particular lived contexts" not as some distant and "ghostly voices refracted through disembodied ideas."[22] The younger history of the UCA (though from various longer ecclesial histories) offers a ripe space to engage with this. Moreover, what spaces are created to enable us to listen to the diversity of voices past and present?

A closer look at the roles associated with deacons, priests and bishops from a postcolonial optic raises further and related questions. While efforts are made to locate shepherding within the context of mutuality and love, a postcolonial perspective will query how "authority" in the life of the Anglican ecclesial tradition has been practised in reality, given that in the liturgical rite of ordination authority is framed in terms of accepting and living by the discipline of the church, and in the context of responsibility pertaining to the refutation of wrong teachings or doctrines. Hence, one of the questions that can be explored is to what extent is the pledge to be faithful to practices of the church geared towards conformity, shuts down conversation of multiple voices and views and perpetuates exclusionary practices? One of the ways by which a colonial/imperial agenda is maintained is through authority that is regulated or managed by bestowing the right to do so on selected individuals or group of individuals and by asserting their authenticity/credibility via a rite (such as ordination) that is linked to a very early historical tradition. Further, the "recruitment of divine elected status simultaneously legitimizes their tenure of power and at the same time inhibits any rumblings toward a counter narrative." In this situation what is seen as a threat are "unscripted inventions and improvisations."[23] What is not given consideration is the fact that this tradition would have been arrived at through the interacting or hybridization of various liturgical impulses of early Christian communities heavily influenced by cultural and ideological factors. Here Sugirtharajah's challenge is timely. He suggests the need for a "widening understanding of the milieu of early Christianity" that will "look beyond the limitations of the Jewish-Hellenistic context" and consider "the Jewish-Aramaic" milieu of early Christianity.[24]

Perhaps the UCA rites can offer some insights to this conversation. While a similar query can be raised about its understanding and employment of authority, one can sense in the dialectic of relational mutuality between lay and ordained that there seems to be, in the UCA rites, more ambivalence with regard to authority. Ambivalence here (as noted below) affords an interesting way to subvert authoritarian tendencies. Likewise, the UCA through its uniting brings together in a creative interplay various histories and ecclesial/ theological ethos. In other words diversity, hybridity and multiple interplays are part and parcel of the life of this tradition. Hence, it is not surprising that the UCA's rites of ordination expose the myth of a "pure and right" rite by creatively blending elements from various ecclesial traditions (both dominant and marginal).

The other problematic is related both to the images (shepherd and servant) and the inherent gradation in the threefold ministry. While the rite(s) suggest a degree of mutuality in terms of relationship and how authority should be employed, we are keenly aware of a degree of ambivalence. Is it that the rite of ordination *vis à vis* the threefold ministry is actually caught between both imperial intentions/ association and praxiological ordering of ministry? Hence, while the rites display elements of managing of power and election under the guise of both divine and historical authority, it is also evident that the rites demonstrate the capacity to embody postcolonial stirrings by focusing responsibility of the ordained on the poor, oppressed and marginalized and especially as the notion of authority is helpfully juxtaposed alongside the rite of foot-washing. It is not insignificant that the empire's limit is also located in the reality of such ambivalence. Thus Homi Bhabha reminds us of the subverting role of ambivalence (and mimicry) in the colonial agenda in the very way it "poses an immanent threat to both 'normalized' knowledges and disciplinary powers."[25] It may be helpful to bear this postcolonial strategy of ambivalence in mind when interrogating ordination rites. For, while the rites do not work on the premise of subverting colonial inclinations, one can already find within them subversive elements that engender complex spaces to resist. This may be the case especially with the UCA rites, but it is also there in the Anglican rites.

Training for Ministry: Postcolonial Perspectives

In this final section of the chapter,[26] we turn attention to questions concerned with training persons for ordained ministry. How would training begin to embrace postcolonial perspectives which would allow concerns like those expressed in this book to surface?

The ordination charge to both deacons and ministers of the Word in the Uniting Church in Australia includes this statement:

> you will announce the good news of God in Christ to those beyond the community of faith, stand alongside those who suffer, and work for justice and peace in the world.[27]

Ordination rites in other settings, and in other traditions, oftentimes make a similar statement about the work of the ordained involving "work for justice." Here, then, is a minimal beginning by which postcolonial optics on the work of ministry might be welcomed.

To propose some postcolonial perspectives on formation for ministry is, however, to be conscious of some possible pre-fixes to "formation": in-formation, con-formation, re-formation, and mal-formation – each in their own way can be drawn into the point that formation is vulnerable to different kinds of suspicion. Information may seem at first to be the relatively neutral term in this cluster, although what we suppose to be information is by no means an unproblematic or value-free notion. Conformation can be deadening, achieved by means of the worst kinds of nastiness that human beings can inflict on one another. And while, in some circumstances, reformation might be judged necessary in order to

guard life-giving matters deemed to be at stake, in other circumstances a hanker for reform might amount to little more than
preoccupation with one's own heady obsessions. The dangers of
malformation need no elaboration (nor do those of an even stronger
word: "de-formation").

It is with caution about how formation can be allied to suspect
motives and practices that we attempt now to draw on Musa Dube's
work on "curriculum transformation" which suggests to us a particular
way of refracting the cluster of prefixes just mentioned, and which
can help us probe how information might relate to conformation, or
to reformation or malformation, or indeed how the prefixes might
be allied in any number of combinations.

Dube's essay is, in our estimation, a most significant challenge to
theological institutions to decolonize their programmes of study. The
challenge has manifold aspects when stretched beyond Dube's own
immediate concern with curriculum to the wider formational work
of theological colleges and seminaries. And its thrust is especially
challenging in supposedly progressive institutions – such as the
Queen's Foundation where we the present authors were colleagues,
and United Theological College, where one is now based – in that
it unflinchingly threatens to reveal "sticking-points," as it were,
where progressive rhetoric is unable to be transformed into practices
that might best manifest conviction about inclusiveness and equal
opportunity.

Dube's essay, "Curriculum Transformation: Dreaming of Decolonization in Theological Studies" is a kind of extended meditation on
R. S. Sugirtharajah's call to theologians to "address the relation
between European expansion and the rise of their own discipline,"[28]
and is found in a Festschrift presented to Sugirtharajah. Sugirtharajah
calls English theologians especially to work on "theological critique
of the empire."[29]

As one of the present authors is English, Dube's challenge is
one we embrace, not least because of conviction, articulated by
Daniel Smith-Christopher, that to be silent in the face of awareness
is to choose complicity. It is a temptation perhaps often faced by
White liberals,[30] and one which is readily institutionalized in liberal
education in White-majority settings – a point Dube makes with
fierce clarity.

In her own elaboration of her opening quotation from Sugirtharajah, Dube has her own strong take on how so much theology "relegate[s] the Other to well-guarded ideological spaces."[31] She speaks from experience of spells at the University of Botswana, Durham University, at two esteemed institutions in the USA (Vanderbilt University, Tennessee and the Claremont Colleges, California) and at the Geneva-based World Council of Churches, before returning to the University of Botswana, this time as teacher. She speaks from experience not only of this study in three continents, but also work with the World Council of Churches, and efforts to raise pan-African church consciousness of issues around AIDS. So she warns of ways in which terms – like "developed" and "developing" – can be "normalized" in everyday conversation,[32] and she notes how talk about "two-thirds world" and "third world" relates to global space. In terms of the curriculum, she observes, perspectives from the so-called two-thirds world and third world are highly unlikely to occupy two thirds of the curriculum anywhere in the world, while everywhere in the world first-world perspectives seem to and do invade much more curricula space than is justified by the recognition that they can at best represent one-third of persons across the planet.[33]

Dube challenges such "colonizing discourse" in the curriculum and is critical of ways in which such discourse, and the invasive practice it symbolizes and galvanizes, infects many "academic canons." These things happen, she notes, even in places where rhetoric of inclusive language and equal opportunity may be firmly in place – and which by implication ought perhaps to know better. So Dube asks, cuttingly: do commitments to equal opportunities and inclusive language translate into disavowal of colonizing ideologies? Why not? If not, how deep does inclusivity run; how pervasive is concern for equality? If theologians are seriously to stretch into active attempts to ditch colonizing ideologies, she identifies that "individual commitment, accountable solidarity, academic leadership and institutional commitment to curriculum transformation"[34] will need to come into play – and all together at once. She is not naïve.

Signs that movement in what she regards as the right direction are taking place will be that Eurocentric (and by extension North Atlantic) theologies will be given less curriculum space. So she laments ways in which her own initial education in theology in

Botswana was preoccupied with the thought of Tillich, Bonhoeffer, Moltmann, Barth, and Vatican II (a concoction of twentieth-century theology that from this list sounds like the one likely to be imbibed in the UK – as David Ford's *Modern Theologians* might suggest). But, Dube says, a stronger sign will be as and when faculties come to be composed of persons who have been educated outside western academic centres.[35]

One of the most challenging features of Dube's essay is the way that her "contribution to the quest" to decolonize the curriculum involves her narrating aspects of her own experiences of studying and teaching theology. She suggests that theologians – and in the light of her opening quotation from Sugirtharajah about English theologians, especially English theologians – need to articulate their own stories, interrogate their own training, and scrutinize the contents of courses they have tried to teach.

Of major significance in our own response to this challenge is the observation that for one of the current authors – Stephen Burns – he experienced having a number of Black and Asian colleagues (including Michael Jagessar, in Birmingham) after having had no Black or Asian lecturers in over a decade of theological study in institutions that no doubt considered themselves progressive. Still, Dube's challenge can be engaged perhaps more deeply by consideration of how he attempted to teach Christian worship, and so the next stretch of reflections in this chapter considers Stephen Burns's introductory worship course at the time we shared work together, and which is represented by *Liturgy* (SCM Studyguide), which relates at least part of what was covered in classrooms at Queen's.[36] As such, this section is an extension of the biographical material in Chapter 1, above.

As a foundational course on worship, Stephen Burns's course "Liturgical Theology and Practice" was part of what is sometimes readily identified as "formational" for ministry. It included some explicit attention to postcolonial perspectives on worship – within sessions on "worship and mission in a diverse world" that looked at a range of contemporary challenges to celebration of "building-blocks" in liturgy. The course was, therefore, constructed around an opening strand of material about "shaping" liturgical experience – the building-blocks – using juxtapositions that are central to liturgical theological method. So, word and sacrament, space and symbol, music and song, preaching and response were paired. Later in the course, other pairings occurred: notably, seasons and cycles, with the whole held within a pair: participating and presiding. By beginning with "word and sacrament," the course began with what are oftentimes called the "central things" of Christian worship,[37] which inevitably led to the depiction of other matters as peripheral to one degree or another.

Exploration of some postcolonial perspectives led to the initial shared writing by the two present authors,[38] and in *Liturgy* such perspectives were considered alongside shifts to directory provisions of liturgical materials, use of new technologies, the inclusion of children, so-called "all-age" worship, feminist, queer, and other sub-cultural challenges. The relevant part of *Liturgy* is headed "Styles and Substance," making the point that different styles of worship have merit – "substance" – which invite exploration. In part, various challenges were clustered to give them a combined force: liturgical studies is particularly susceptible to working with heavy and inflexible notions of tradition, and it certainly seems to be the case that some liturgists are quicker to acknowledge the fragmentariness of Christian liturgical origins than they are to bless and relish contemporary diversity in Christian worship.

One review of the book that emerged from some of this material described the section on postcolonial and other challenges as a "whirlwind," while another dismissed it as a pointless foray into "passing fads"![39] The latter response, especially, is interesting if only in that it suggests just how strange such perspectives may be to some and how much energy might need to be expended to create even small space for postcolonial perspectives to be heard in certain circles.

Throughout the course, there was an attempt to take care to constantly keep on using juxtapositions and the ways that they can resist closure and singularity, to beckon a kind of spaciousness in which different voices might be raised. But still, it remains the case that the course clustered various optics – around ethnicity, gender and sexual orientation, for example – which can all too easily suggest a homogenization which either may or may not be there depending on all kinds of particularities.

As teaching of the course over time developed, so did moves intentionally to destabilize normative orders of encounter with material.
So, for example, in later experience of teaching this course, rather
than tracing trajectories in eucharistic prayer through the *Didache* and
Apostolic Tradition, to *Addai and Mari*, and ambling on apparently
historically, the course began by looking at things like the Zaire
Mass (an inculturated liturgy that has proved deeply problematic for
the Roman hierarchy), and prayers and gestures from a eucharistic
community that worships in a gay bar, and at which a drag queen
presides. On the one hand, of course these are in the scheme of
things very small moves, entirely inadequate to the wholesale transformation of curricula that would be required if Dube's dreams are
to be realized, let alone stretched again beyond curricula to encircle
everything involved in participation in a community of formation.
Yet they do, we suggest, at least begin, in their own small ways,
to point to shifts that need to take place in at least the part of the
curriculum concerned with liturgical studies if postcolonial perspectives are to find a space that can be enlarged to engage them more
adequately. So, on the other hand, small gains may be the start of
larger changes. And lovers of liturgy especially might agree with the
assertion that gestures are important.[40]

Concluding Observations:
Rethinking Tradition

There are many loose ends in our conversation, but in attempting to contend with texts, symbols, song, scripture, time, space, and certain rites relating to persons, we have at least attempted to begin a conversation – one we ourselves think is, and we hope others will judge to be – worth pursuing. Among the loose ends, we have chosen to conclude with a brief reflection on one strand of our thinking that has run as an undercurrent throughout the preceding chapters, and which we consider to be of major relevance: what postcolonial perspectives on Christian worship might offer to rethinking the notion, use and usefulness of "tradition." In this regard we agree with Jione Havea that "[t]o arrest the colonial legacy, we must be critical of mainline (or man-line) traditions, experiences and reasons": our project is not merely about displacement. It calls for "supplementation and transformation" as well. Havea locates such an undertaking in "two interconnected moves": "critique the mainline (hermeneutics of suspicion) and making room for the sidelined (hermeneutics of identification and of retrieval)."[1]

Rethinking Tradition

David Lowenthal, in *The Past is a Foreign Country*, notes the following: "reverence for tradition underlies destructive iconoclasm."[2] His fundamental point in this volume is that humans always wish to relive and repossess the past as if it was good, though it was not necessarily so. In a nutshell, humans tend to be "antiquarians" idealizing the cultural and religious productions of the past – wishing to collect them. Certainly, in Christian worship and the production of liturgical texts, the accusation of "antiquarianism" only partly fits – for the very proliferation of new texts and resources in this realm suggests a very lively contemporary scene. Still, appeal to the antique is an important feature in the judgment of many persons, groups and denominations about what kinds of worship bear authority, or are considered most worthy. So the past and the present are closely woven: movements of liturgical renewal oftentimes appeal to the past as they seek to work on present productions. Hence, Lowenthal problematizes a fundamental task that is part of a postcolonial critique of Christian worship, as indeed any other approach to discernment in liturgical celebration: What actually informed and shaped the theological presuppositions of the liturgical productions of the past? In our concluding reflections, we note that while appeals to the antique are prevalent, and no doubt important, in liturgical studies and liturgical practice, such appeals rarely make connections between ritual and textual productions and empire.

It is of course the case that tradition has always played a determining role in theological understanding and liturgical practices, despite the fact that this is not always overtly acknowledged. Even the Brethren, for example, have their tradition, and as with any other Christian group, it determines what is made of scripture and any other acknowledged sources of authority, no matter what claims may be made about the primacy of the Bible or whatever else. If we can assent to the definition of theology as *fides quaerens intellectus*, that is, faith seeking understanding, it is impossible – and dishonest – to contend that the "intellectus" is value-free and unmediated in the process of learning. Tradition has to be "incarnated," as well as to a great degree syncretistic – borrowing from contexts and cultures in its meaning-making. Further, tradition is that which evolves or is handed over/down.

Our agenda, a self-consciously subjective take which has attempted to engage, represent and apply a range of scholarship, has been to interrogate and expose imperial impulses that may be linked to liturgical rites or worship within Christian traditions. Our fundamental quarrel is with certain ways in which tradition has been received, accepted and remains largely un-interrogated. Hence our questions:

1. How do we negotiate both openness to tradition and a commitment to subject it to questions in the light of colonial, postcolonial and contemporary concerns?

2. Is tradition to hand, and to hand on, as if written on granite? And in what ways is it more malleable?

3. How are suggestions of a singular tradition to be broken open and fragmented, not least to reveal perspectives "from the underside" of majority perspectives, the smothering of difference through "orthodox" consensus, or sheer brutal yielding of power by some groups over others?

4. How is discernment to be made about what facets of tradition are best preserved and which each generation would do well to try to make sense of as their inheritance in whatever is their present?

5. What might we mean when we speak of the "deposit of faith"? Why – and in what ways – should tradition determine faith for future generations?

We are acutely aware – and perhaps to a different extent, appreciative – of the tendency to affirm the capacity of tradition itself to act as a critical voice (or a cacophony of critical voices) that can counter contemporary perspectives to which persons might otherwise become captive to (or tunnel-visioned by). We are also aware that we constantly need to consider and revise our assumptions about tradition. Even "good things" about tradition – such as the capacity to critique the narrowly contemporary – need to be subject to some forceful basic questions, most notably for instance, "what do we mean by tradition" and "whose tradition"? Questions about how traditions other than those that came to be dominant might be heard or reconstructed, and how prevailing traditions need to be de-centred and relativized, will have deep consequences for whatever notion of "critical classicism" remains possible – if that notion can or ought to survive at all.

As we have shown in the preceding chapters, postcolonial optics challenge the hegemonic tendencies of tradition and at the same time draw on aspects of tradition – especially subaltern voices and perspectives in tradition. Postcolonial critique of tradition is, therefore, a complex, complicated and compromised undertaking. While there are indeed clear points of contestation and conflict, these are not necessarily straightforward, not least because the world of colonizer and colonized is tied in an interweaving relationship.

The prospect of re-reading, re-writing and re-constructing tradition is a great challenge for those that in one way or another "gate-keep" particular perspectives on tradition in order to ensure their own survival and retention of power. In the face of this, in this book we have attempted to problematize the notion of tradition premised on authoritative liturgical texts and to raise awareness of the dangers of ideological and hegemonic motivation associated with much inherited tradition that remains un-deconstructed and un-interrogated and which continues to silence dissenting voices.

Tradition is not value free. Conceptions of tradition in the history of the Christian church are enmeshed in power-plays that envelop the history of empire, and which shape our intellectual pursuits and our personal self-understanding at the deepest level. This dynamic is of course reflected in our liturgical texts and practices. If the practices, symbols and texts that combine in rites define who we are as Christians, then it is imperative that they are subject to scrutiny in order to understand ourselves and our own theological presupposi-tions and theological constructions.

Interrogation of tradition(s) is necessarily a critical scrutiny of the past. Yet, it is more than that. In the literary field, Talal Asad helpfully elaborates: "Criticisms of the past," he writes,

> are morally relevant only when the past still informs the present – when contemporaries invoke the authority of founding ancestors against each other. In criticizing the dead, one is therefore questioning what they have authorized in the living.[3]

When texts from the past (our tradition) still continue hegemoni-cally to form and inform contemporary liturgical acts without those who engage those acts being aware of the outmoded world and structures from which these rites have come, it is high time for critical reflections. Hence we offer a timely reminder from the late Edward Said:

> Appeals to the past are among the commonest strategies in interpreta-tions of the present. What animates such appeals is not only disagreement about what happened in the past and what the past was, but uncertainty about whether the past really is past, over and concluded, or whether it continues, albeit in different forms, perhaps.[4]

As we have noted earlier, the Latin word from which we receive the English "tradition" not only means to deliver, surrender, transmit or handover. It also means "treason," that is, to hand someone over to an enemy by fraud. The meanings of tradition therefore embrace poignant ambiguities. We have been keen to underscore not only the dynamic nature of tradition, but to locate its dynamism in its ambiguities. We perceive a relationship between tradition and subversion that engenders handing over or passing on, but not so as to prescribe and bring closure on insights. Our project affirms the capacity of key components of liturgical tradition to promote human flourishing: bringing durable critical resources to bear on the merely contemporary or parochial quirkiness of individuals in all their tendencies to tyranny; enabling desire for justice and beatitude; and mediating an empowering sense of divine presence, not least among those in whom others have failed to trace the full strength of the *imago dei*. None of this is to be underestimated. Moreover, we affirm the capacity of liturgical tradition to surface perspectives that can subvert the liturgical tradition, thereby stumping up strong correctives to its own trajectories that stand in need of reconsideration.

Appreciation of the ambiguities of liturgical tradition is able to enlarge capacity both to dislodge and to begin to reconfigure so-called mainstream – perhaps oppressive – employment of the tradition. The tradition itself yields resources that question and challenge its own development, and which interrogate as well as complexify and complement predominant and popular (in different senses) themes within itself. Tradition is therefore rightly described as "living" in that it is to some extent flexible and so capable of its own redefinition and transformation. It is thereby also always to some extent provisional, being populated with counter-voices and contra-dictoriness. Affirmation of tradition therefore entails the celebration of the "counter, original, spare, [and] strange"[5] which is part of its own identity. Such a view is crucial, we propose, if appeal to tradition is not to become a tool to enforce uniformity and the subjugation of minorities to majorities. Perhaps convictions about tradition that do not mediate a strong sense of strangeness are not reliable in their insights, and at best represent partial local memory?

One crucial dimension of these affirmations is a clear-eyed courage to name ways in which tradition has been, and continues to be, employed as a weapon of oppression. We have tried not to shy away from this. Indeed, in our lack of shyness we admit that it is possible that at times we are wrong – at least perhaps overstated, exaggerated – about some, though not all, of the details and nuances we have attempted to explore in this book. We nevertheless affirm that we indeed are quite right to insist, repeatedly, on one of our central convictions: that living tradition requires inclusion of subaltern and excluded voices. Our postcolonial perspectives should therefore fund the critical dimensions of any critical classicist approach to liturgical studies, as well, we believe, as constituting that classicism by celebrating how subaltern optics have and might yet shape the tradition itself in enlarged ways.[6]

So it is by no means that we are dismissing tradition. On the contrary, our whole project has been premised on the rediscovery of varied richness, or as Joerg Rieger puts it, the "surpluses" of multivalent Christian traditions. Yet this demands critical interrogation. As Joerg Rieger writes:

> The constructive task depends on the analytical one. Without understanding how we are shaped by empire all the way into our deepest desires, we cannot properly identify the theological surplus, those intuitions and insights that point us beyond the horizons of empire... Without the analytical exploration of theology and empire we will not be able to identify what is really path-breaking in theology, what it is that has the potential to shape truly fresh and constructive thinking about God and the world.[7]

About the Authors

Michael N. Jagessar is Secretary for Racial Justice and Multicultural Ministry for the United Reformed Church, UK. From 2012 Michael will serve as moderator of the General Assembly of the United Reformed Church. His publications include *Postcolonial Black British Theology: New Textures and Themes* (co-edited with Anthony G. Reddie, Epworth Press, 2007), *Black Theology in Britain: A Reader* (co-edited with Anthony G. Reddie, Equinox, 2007), and *The Edge of God: New Liturgical Texts and Contexts in Conversation* (co-edited with Nicola Slee and Stephen Burns, Epworth Press, 2008). He is book reviews editor of *Black Theology: An International Journal.*

Stephen Burns is Research Fellow in Public and Contextual Theology, United Theological College, Charles Sturt University, Australia. His publications include *Worship in Context: Liturgical Theology, Children and the City* (Epworth Press, 2006), *Liturgy* (SCM Press, 2006), *Exchanges of Grace: Essays in Honour of Ann Loades* (co-edited with Natalie K. Watson, SCM Press, 2008), *The Edge of God: New Liturgical Texts and Contexts in Conversation* (co-edited with Nicola Slee and Michael Jagessar, Epworth Press, 2008), *Christian Worship in Australia: Inculturating the Liturgical Tradition* (co-edited with Anita Monro, St Pauls, 2009) and *Presiding Like a Woman* (co-edited with Nicola Slee, SPCK, 2010). He is book reviews editor of *Australian Journal of Liturgy* and a member of the Uniting Church in Australia's national Assembly Working Group on Worship.

Notes

Preface

1. Stephen Burns, Nicola Slee and Michael N. Jagessar (eds), *The Edge of God: New Liturgical Texts and Contexts in Conversation* (Peterborough: Epworth Press, 2008).
2. David F. Ford, *The Modern Theologians* (Oxford: Blackwell, in three editions – 1989, 1997, 2005). Each edition has employed variant subtitles; the first edition was published in two volumes, the second and third in one large book; the third edition is edited with Rachel Muers.
3. Daniel W. Hardy and David F. Ford, *Jubilate: Theology in Praise* (London: Darton, Longman and Todd, 1984), republished in an amended version as David F. Ford and Daniel W. Hardy, *Living in Praise: Worshipping and Knowing God* (London: Darton, Longman and Todd, 2005). Note also Ford's reflection on worship in his *The Shape of Living* (London: Fount, 1997) and *Self and Salvation: Being Transformed* (Cambridge: Cambridge University Press, 1999).

Garibay: *In his Image*

1. http://www.emmanuelgaribay.com/mginhisimagesm.jpg
2. Derek Walcott, "The Sea is History," in his *Collected Poems 1948–1984* (London: Faber & Faber, 1986), 364–67.
3. Kamau Brathwaite, "History, the Caribbean Writer, and X/Self," in Geoffrey Davies and Hena Maes-Jelinek (eds), *Crisis and Creativity in the New Literatures in English* (Amsterdam: Rodopi, 1990), 23–45.
4. David Philippart, *Saving Signs, Wondrous Words* (Chicago: Liturgy Training Publications, 1996), 9.
5. Perhaps the best known is shown in Michelle P. Brown, *Christian Art* (London: Lion, 2008), 406. Another version is at: http://amistad-vacaville.org/garibay.htm
6. http://amistad-vacaville.org/Comments.htm
7. See http://www.emmanuelgaribay.com/theologiansmall.jpg. Garibay's image entitled "Theologian" shows a naked reader – also bespectacled – surrounded by symbols, some of them ominous.

8. This quotation comes from paragraph 103 of Blessed Joron of Saxony's *Libellus*, accessible in various forms in print and electronic media, with the quote itself accessible in Robert Atwell, *Celebrating the Saints* (Norwich: Canterbury Press, 1998), 254.

Introduction

1. This college was originally founded as a College for Medicine and the study of theology and was named Queen's College. After the medical school was moved to another location and became part of the University of Birmingham (Queen's nearest neighbour), Queen's College only focused on theological education and ministerial formation.

2. Modules include: Liberation Theologies, Black and Asian Theologies, Feminist and Womanist Theologies, Exploring and Celebrating Differences, Interfaith Studies, Bible and Liberation, Black Theology and Christian Formation, and Bible and Interpretive Optics.

3. Musa Dube, "Curriculum Transformation: Dreaming of Decolonization in Theological Studies," in D. N. Premnath (ed.), *Border Crossings: Cross-Cultural Hermeneutics. Essays in Honor of R. S. Sugirtharajah* (Maryknoll, NY: Orbis Books, 2007), 121–38 (125).

4. R. S. Sugirtharajah, *The Postcolonial Biblical Reader* (Oxford: Blackwell, 2006), 18–19. This point is also made by Michael N. Jagessar and Anthony G. Reddie in their *Black Theology in Britain: A Reader* (London: Equinox, 2007). Michael Jagessar also made this point in his article "Navigating the World of 'White Ecumenism': Insights from Philip Potter," *Wereld en Zending* 31.4 (2002): 32–41.

5. Diana Eck, "Prospects for Pluralism: Voice and Vision in the Study of Religion," *Journal of the American Academy of Religion* 75.4 (2007): 743–76 (753).

6. Anthony G. Reddie, *Nobodies to Somebodies: A Practical Theology for Education and Liberation* (Peterborough: Epworth Press, 2003).

7. Homi Bhabha, *The Location of Culture* (London: Routledge, 1994), 4.

8. Mayra Rivera, *The Touch of Transcendence: A Postcolonial Theology of God* (Louisville, KY: Westminster John Knox Press, 2007), 10.

9. Gordon W. Lathrop, *Holy Things: A Liturgical Theology* (Minneapolis, MN: Fortress Press, 1993), 4–5.

10. Massimo Leone, *Religious Conversion and Identity: The Semiotic Analysis of Texts* (London: Routledge, 2004), 54.

Chapter 1

1. See Daniel Smith-Christopher, "Abolitionist Exegesis: A Quaker Proposal for White Liberals," in R. S. Sugitharajah (ed.), _Still at the Margins: Biblical Scholarship Fifteen Years After Voices from the Margins_ (London: T&T Clark, 2008), 128–38 (133).

2. See Gail Ramshaw on liturgical language "stuttering" to say God in _Reviving Sacred Speech: The Meaning of Liturgical Language_, 2nd edn (Akron, OH: OSL Publications, 2000), 29.

3. See R. S. Sugirtharajah, "Muddling Along at the Margins," in R. S. Sugitharajah (ed.), _Still at the Margins: Biblical Scholarship Fifteen Years After Voices from the Margins_ (London: T&T Clark, 2008), 8–21 (11).

4. Sugirtharajah, "Muddling Along," 12.

5. Sugirtharajah, "Muddling Along," 12.

6. Sugirtharajah, "Muddling Along," 11.

7. Lathrop, _Holy Things_, 4–5.

8. See Ann Loades, _Searching for Lost Coins_ (London: SPCK, 1987). See also Natalie K. Watson and Stephen Burns (eds), _Exchanges of Grace: Essays in Honour of Ann Loades_ (London: SCM Press, 2008).

9. Dolores S. Williams, _Sisters in the Wilderness: The Challenge of Womanist God-talk_ (Maryknoll, NY: Orbis Books, 1993), ix.

10. Emmanuel Lartey, _In Living Colour: An Intercultural Approach to Pastoral Care and Counselling_ (London: Cassell, 1997), 12.

11. A caveat in terms of my interest in this conversation is both necessary and appropriate. I am a Caribbean theologian by training with a keen interest in Caribbean culture, identity, religions and literature. My MA research is in the area of theology and Caribbean literature (specifically the works of Wilson Harris) and my PhD work on a life and work of a Caribbean theologian (Philip Potter), the first Black leader of the World Council of Churches. I taught Interfaith and Ecumenical Studies, Black and Asian Theologies and Postcolonial Biblical Hermeneutics.

12. See Donna E. Schaper, _Raising Interfaith Children: Spiritual Orphans or Spiritual Heirs?_ (New York: Crossroad, 1999).

13. See Michael N. Jagessar, "The Sacred in Caribbean Literature: A Theological Conversation," in Dawn Llewellyn and Deborah F. Sawyer (eds), _Reading Spiritualities: Constructing and Representing the Sacred_ (Aldershot: Ashgate, 2008), 27–50.

14. See Michael N. Jagessar, "Spinning Theology: Trickster, Texts and Theology," in Michael N. Jagessar and Anthony G. Reddie (eds), _Postcolonial Black British Theology: New Textures and Themes_ (Peterborough: Epworth Press, 2007), 124–46.

15. Paul Heelas, Linda Woodhead _et al._, _The Spiritual Revolution: Why Religion is Giving Way to Spirituality_ (Oxford: Blackwell, 2005).

16. See Stephen Burns, "Forgiveness in Challenging Circumstances," in Fraser Watts and Elizabeth Gulliford (eds), *Forgiveness in Context: Theology and Psychology in Creative Dialogue* (London: Continuum, 2004), 144–59.

17. See Stephen Burns, *Worship in Context: Liturgical Theology, Children and the City* (Peterborough: Epworth Press, 2006).

18. For a brief reflection, see Stephen Burns, *Welcoming Asylum Seekers* (Cambridge: Grove Books, 2004).

19. See Stephen Burns, *Liturgy* (SCM Studyguide) (London: SCM Press, 2006) which is related to liturgy as it was taught at Queen's.

20. Kwok Pui-lan, "The Legacy of Cultural Hegemony in the Anglican Church," in Ian T. Douglas and Kwok Pui-lan (eds), *Beyond Colonial Anglicanism: The Anglican Communion in the Twenty-First Century* (New York: Church Publishing, 2001), 47–70 (59).

21. Pui-lan, "The Legacy of Cultural Hegemony," 59–60.

22. Kwok Pui-lan, "Theology and Social Theory," in Kwok Pui-lan, Don H. Compier and Joerg Rieger (eds), *Empire and the Christian Tradition: New Readings of Classical Theologians* (Minneapolis, MN: Fortress Press, 2007), 15–29 (19).

23. Pui-lan, "The Legacy of Cultural Hegemony," 65.

24. For a large recent study, see Pui-lan, Compier and Rieger (eds), *Empire and the Christian Tradition: New Readings of Classical Theologians* (Minneapolis, MN: Fortress Press, 2007).

25. Joerg Rieger, "Christian Theology and Empires," in Kwok Pui-lan, Don H. Compier and Joerg Rieger (eds), *Empire and the Christian Tradition: New Readings of Classical Theologians* (Minneapolis, MN: Fortress Press, 2007), 1–13 (13).

26. Idris Hamid, *In Search of New Perspectives* (Trinidad: CCC, 1972), 8.

27. See Stephen Burns and Anita Monro (eds), *Christian Worship in Australia: Inculturating the Liturgical Tradition* (Strathfield, NSW: St Pauls, 2009).

28. Rieger, "Christian Theology and Empires," 1.

29. R. S. Sugirtharajah, *Postcolonial Reconfigurations: An Alternative Way of Reading the Bible and Doing Theology* (London: SCM Press, 2003), 2.

30. See Bill Ashcroft, Gareth Griffiths and Helen Tiffin, *The Postcolonial Studies Reader* (New York: Routledge, 1995). Also, for a fine essay on the development of the term, see Fernando F. Segovia, "Mapping the Postcolonial Optic in Biblical Criticism: Meaning and Scope," in Stephen C. Moore and Fernando F. Segovia (eds), *Postcolonial Biblical Criticism: Interdisciplinary Intersections* (London: T&T Clark, 2005), 23–78.

31. The following works are helpful in giving an overview of the relationship between postcolonial criticism, biblical studies, and theology: R. S. Sugirtharajah, *The Bible and the Third World: Precolonial, Colonial and Postcolonial Encounters* (Cambridge: Cambridge University Press, 2001);

R. S. Sugirtharajah, *Postcolonial Criticism and Biblical Interpretation* (Oxford: Oxford University Press, 2002); Laura Donaldson and Kwok Pui-lan (eds), *Postcolonialism, Feminism and Religious Discourse* (New York: Routledge, 2002); Musa Dube, *Postcolonial Feminist Interpretation of the Bible* (St. Louis, MO: Chalice Press, 2000); Kwok Pui-lan, *Postcolonial Imagination and Feminist Theology* (Louisville, KY: Westminster John Knox Press, 2005); Wonhee Anne Joh, *Heart of the Cross: A Postcolonial Christology* (Louisville, KY: Westminster John Knox Press, 2006); Joerg Rieger, *Christ and Empire: From Paul to Postcolonial Times* (Minneapolis, MN: Fortress Press, 2007); Kwok Pui-lan, Don H. Compier and Joerg Rieger (eds), *Empire and the Christian Tradition: New Readings of Classical Theologians* (Minneapolis, MN: Fortress Press, 2007).

32. Sugirtharajah, *Postcolonial Reconfigurations*, 4.

33. Bhabha, *The Location of Cultures*.

34. Pui-lan, "The Legacy of Cultural Hegemony," 53–54.

35. R. S. Sugirtharajah, "The First, Second and Third Letters of John," in R. S. Sugirtharajah (ed.), *A Postcolonial Commentary on the New Testament Writings* (London: T&T Clark, 2007), 413–23 (413).

36. Pui-lan, "Theology and Social Theory," 19.

37. Pui-lan, "Theology and Social Theory," 20

38. Pui-lan, "Theology and Social Theory," 21.

39. Christopher Duraisingh, "Towards a Postcolonial Re-Visioning of the Church's Faith, Witness and Communion," in Ian T. Douglas and Kwok Pui-lan (eds), *Beyond Colonial Anglicanism* (New York: Church Publishing, 2001), 337–67 (337).

40. Duraisingh, "Towards a Postcolonial Re-Visioning," 345.

41. Duraisingh, "Towards a Postcolonial Re-Visioning," 347; original emphasis.

42. See Jeffrey L. Staley, " 'Dis Place Man': A Postcolonial Critique of the Vine (the Mountain and the Temple) in the Gospel of John," in Musa Dube and Jeffrey L. Staley (eds), *John and Postcolonialism: Travel, Space and Power* (London: Sheffield Academic Press, 2002), 32–50.

43. R. S. Sugirtharajah, "Postcolonial and Biblical Interpretation: The Next Phase," in R. S. Sugirtharajah (ed.), *A Postcolonial Commentary on the New Testament* (London: T&T Clark, 2005), 455–66 (465).

44. Dwight W. Vogel (ed.), *Primary Sources in Liturgical Theology: A Reader* (Collegeville, MN: Liturgical Press, 2000).

45. Paul F. Bradshaw, *The Search for the Origins of Christian Worship*, 2nd edn (London: SPCK, 2002).

46. Paul F. Bradshaw, *Eucharistic Origins* (London: SPCK, 2004).

47. See Geoffrey Wainwright, *Worship With One Accord: Where Liturgy and Ecumenism Embrace* (Oxford: Oxford University Press, 1997).

48. See Thomas F. Best and Dagmar Heller (eds), *Worship Today: Understanding, Practice, Ecumenical Implications* (Geneva: World Council of Churches, 2004).

49. Walter Brueggemann, *Texts under Negotiation: The Bible and Postmodern Imagination* (Minneapolis, MN: Fortress Press, 1993), 19–20. The latter emphasis is ours.

50. Diana Bryden and Helen Tiffin, *Decolonising Fictions* (Denmark: Dangaroo Press, 1993), 26.

Chapter 2

1. This foundational chapter is closely related to our material published in *Worship* 80 (2006): 428–52 and *Black Theology: An International Journal* 5 (2007): 39–62.

2. R. S. Sugirtharajah, *Postcolonial Reconfigurations: An Alternative Way of Reading the Bible and Doing Theology* (London: SCM Press, 2003), 143.

3. Examples include: Musa Dube, *Postcolonial Feminist Interpretation of the Bible* (St. Louis, MO: Chalice Press, 2000); Musa Dube and Jeffrey L. Staley, *John and Postcolonialism: Travel, Space and Power* (London: Sheffield Academic Press, 2002); Fernando Segovia, *Interpreting Beyond Borders* (London: Sheffield Academic Press, 2000); Kwok Pui-lan, *Postcolonial Imagination and Feminist Theology* (London: SCM Press, 2005); R. S. Sugirtharajah (ed.), *The Postcolonial Bible* (London: Sheffield Academic Press, 1998); R. S. Sugirtharajah, *Postcolonial Criticism and Biblical Interpretation* (Oxford: Oxford University Press, 2002); R. S. Sugirtharajah, *Postcolonial Reconfigurations: An Alternative Way of Reading the Bible and Doing Theology* (London: SCM Press, 2003).

4. See Catherine Keller, Michael Nausner and Mayra Rivera (eds), *Postcolonial Theologies: Divinity and Empire* (St. Louis, MO: Chalice Press, 2004); Marion Grau, *Of Divine Economy: Refinancing Redemption* (New York: T&T Clark International, 2004).

5. Paul Bradshaw (ed.), *The New SCM Dictionary of Liturgy and Worship* (London: SCM Press, 2002).

6. Virginia Fabella and R. S. Sugirtharajah (eds), *The SCM Dictionary of Third World Theologies* (London: SCM Press, 2003).

7. Musa Dube, "Reading for Decolonization (John 4:1–42)," in Musa Dube and Jeffrey L. Staley (eds), *John and Postcolonialism: Travel, Space and Power* (London: Sheffield Academic Press, 2002), 51–75 (56).

8. A search of the catalogues of major liturgical publishing houses of liturgical studies also indicates the dearth of attention to postcolonial studies or theory in liturgical studies.

9. See Austin Flannery (ed.), *Vatican Council II: Conciliar and Post-Conciliar Documents* (New York: Costello, 1975).

10. See also his *Cultural Adaptation of the Liturgy* (New York: Paulist Press, 1982); *Liturgical Inculturation: Sacramentals, Religiosity and Catechesis* (Collegeville, MN: Liturgical Press, 1992); and *Liturgies of the Future: The Process and Methods of Inculturation* (Mahwah, NJ: Paulist Press, 1989). In the British context, the recent work of the Anglican liturgist Philip Tovey is important: see his *Inculturation of Christian Worship: Exploring the Eucharist* (Aldershot: Ashgate, 2004). This recently published study, however, includes no sustained engagement with postcolonial literature.

11. Anscar Chupungco, "The Theological Principle of Adaptation," in Dwight Vogel (ed.), *Primary Sources of Liturgical Theology: A Reader* (Collegeville, MN: Liturgical Press, 2000), 247–52 (252).

12. Myke Johnsont, "Wanting to be Indian: When Spiritual Searching Turns into Cultural Theft," in Joanne Pearson (ed.), *Belief Beyond Boundaries: WICCA, Celtic Spirituality and the New Age* (Aldershot: Ashgate, 2005), 277–94 (281). Our addition in brackets.

13. R. S. Sugirtharajah (ed.), *Vernacular Hermeneutics* (Sheffield: Sheffield Academic Press, 1999), 12.

14. Pui-lan, "The Legacy of Cultural Hegemony," 59.

15. See Ian T. Douglas and Kwok Pui-lan (eds), *Beyond Colonial Anglicanism: The Anglican Communion in the Twenty-First Century* (New York: Church Publishing, 2001).

16. For brief but significant critique, see James White, *Protestant Worship: Traditions in Transition* (Louisville, KY: Westminster John Knox Press, 1989), 215, and James White, *Roman Catholic Worship: From Trent to Today* (Mahwah, NJ: Paulist Press, 1995), 143–44. James White is interesting because of both his resistance to liturgical consensus and uniformity. This is most sharply articulated in his article "How Do We Know it is Us?," in E. Byron Anderson and Bruce Morrill (eds), *Liturgy and the Moral Self: Humanity at Full Stretch Before God* (Collegeville, MN: Liturgical Press, 1998), 55–66. His reserve about what inculturation might mean for Christian worship in the context of North American culture, is located in his critique of Willow Creek whose "premises are not all that different from those in use at Mobil Oil headquarters down the road" so that "worshipers must feel as much at home on Sunday just as they do at corporate headquarters on Monday." Furthermore, at Willow Creek, "there is not a single Christian symbol visible." He counsels that, at least in the American context, maybe "it is time to stop theorizing about inculturation. It is here and its results are dramatic" (James F. White, "Protestant Public Worship in America, 1935–1995," in *Christian Worship in North America: A Retrospective, 1955–1995* [Collegeville, MN: Liturgical Press, 1997], 115–33 [132]).

17. See Staley, " 'Dis Place Man'."

18. Mukti Barton, "I am Black and Beautiful," *Black Theology: An International Journal* 2.2 (2004): 167–87 (167). See also Mukti Barton, *Rejection, Resistance, Resurrection: Speaking Out on Racism in the Church* (London: Darton, Longman and Todd, 2005).

19. Barton, "I am Black and Beautiful," 168.

20. Gay L. Byron, *Symbolic Blackness and Ethnic Difference in Early Christian Literature* (London: Routledge, 2002), 50.

21. Robert Hood, *Begrimed and Black: Christian Traditions on Black and Blackness* (London: Routledge, 1994), 90.

22. See Charles Long, *Significations: Signs, Symbols, and Images in the Interpretation of Religion* (Philadelphia, PA: Fortress Press, 1986); Henry Louis Gates, Jr, *The Signifying Monkey: A Theory of Afro-American Literary Criticism* (New York: Oxford University Press, 1988).

23. Dube, "Reading for Decolonization (John 4:1–42)," 56.

24. See Edward Said, *Orientalism: Western Representations of the Orient* (London: Routledge, 1978). Said's monumental work together with Frantz Fanon's writings have greatly influenced postcolonial scholarship. Two other significant voices are Gayatri Chakravorty Spivak and Homi K. Bhabha.

25. See Frantz Fanon, *Black Skin, White Masks* (London: Pluto Press, 1986).

26. Frantz Fanon, *The Wretched of the Earth* (New York: Grove Press, 1965), 37.

27. Gail Ramshaw, *Liturgical Language: Making it Metaphoric, Keeping it Inclusive* (Collegeville, MN: Liturgical Press, 1996), 29.

28. Ramshaw, *Liturgical Language*, 29.

29. Gail Ramshaw, *God Beyond Gender: Feminist Christian God-Language* (Minneapolis, MN: Fortress Press, 1995). See also her *Treasures Old and New: Images in the Lectionary* (Minneapolis, MN: Fortress Press, 2002); *Under the Tree of Life: The Religion of a Feminist Christian* (New York: Continuum, 1999); and *Worship: Searching for Language* (Washington DC: Pastoral Press, 1988), all fine studies of the problems and potential of language used in liturgical contexts.

30. Ramshaw, *Liturgical Language*, 28.

31. Ramshaw, *Liturgical Language*, 29.

32. See the three-volume *Readings for the Assembly*, cycles A, B and C, ed. Gail Ramshaw and Gordon Lathrop (Minneapolis, MN: Fortress Press, 1995–97).

33. Marion Grau, "Divine Commerce: A Postcolonial Christology of the Times of Neocolonial Empire," in Catherine Keller, Michael Nausner and Mayra Rivera (eds), *Postcolonial Theologies: Divinity and Empire* (St. Louis: MO: Chalice Press, 2004), 178–79.

34. Ramshaw, *Liturgical Language*, 30.

35. Said, *Orientalism*, 3.

36. Ramshaw, *Liturgical Language*, 31.

37. John M. Hull, *In the Beginning There was Darkness: A Blind Person's Conversations with the Bible* (London: SCM Press, 2001), esp. 108–113.

38. Ramshaw, *Liturgical Language*, 33–34.

39. Ramshaw, *Liturgical Language*, 33.

40. Iona Community, *The Courage to Say No* (Glasgow: Wild Goose Resources, 1996), hymn 42. Tune: COMPLIMENT, no doubt a play on the "complement" of light and darkness in the text.

41. For author's comment see Graham Kings and Geoff Morgan, *Offerings from Kenya to Anglicanism: Liturgical Texts and Contexts including "A Kenyan Service of Holy Communion"* (Alcuin/GROW Joint Liturgical Study 50) (Cambridge: Grove Books, 2001), 27.

42. Glauco S. de Lima, "Preface," in Ian T. Douglas and Kwok Pui-lan (eds), *Beyond Colonial Anglicanism* (New York: Church Publishing, 2001), 1–8 (3).

43. See Sugirtharajah, *Postcolonial Criticism and Biblical Interpretation*, 79.

44. As in the *Methodist Worship Book* (Peterborough: Methodist Publishing House, 1999), 127, citing the Advent order, although the rubric is included in orders for every season.

45. See, for example, R. C. D. Jasper and G. J. Cuming (eds), *Prayers of the Eucharist: Early and Reformed*, 3rd edn (Collegeville, MN: Liturgical Press, 1987), 282.

46. Barton, "I am Black and Beautiful," esp. 175.

47. We recall Inderjit Bhogal's own common practice of covering the eucharistic elements with a vibrantly coloured cloth that was a gift to him from his own Sikh parents. We note also the practice of the parish of St Gregory of Nyssa, San Francisco, who cover their altar-table (and adorn their persons) with multi-coloured fabric as an expression of welcoming the cultures of the world to their local liturgy. Their practice is illustrated on their website, www.saintgregorys.org, and described by former co-rector Donald Snell in his "Rending the Temple Veil: Holy Space in Holy Community," in John Ander Runckle (ed.), *Searching for Sacred Space: Essays on Architecture and Liturgical Design in the Episcopal Church* (New York: Church Publishing, 2002), 149–81.

48. See Stephen Burns, "Presiding Like a Woman: Feminist Gestures for Christian Assembly," *Feminist Theology* 18 (2009): 32–54.

49. Janet Walton, *Feminist Liturgy: A Matter of Justice* (Collegeville, MN: Liturgical Press, 2000), 37–38.

50. Gayatri Chakravorty Spivak, "Can the Subaltern Speak?" in Cary Nelson and Lawrence Grossberg (eds), *Marxism and the Interpretation of Culture* (Urbana, IL: University of Illinois Press, 1988), 271–313 (306).

51. Margaret Shanti, "Worship/Rituals," in Virginia Fabella and R. S. Sugirtharajah (eds), *The SCM Dictionary of Third World Theologies* (London: SCM Press, 2003), 239.

52. Don E. Saliers, "Towards a Spirituality of Inclusiveness," in Nancy Eisland and Don E. Saliers (eds), *Human Disability and the Service of God: Reassessing Religious Practice* (Nashville, TN: Abingdon Press, 1998), 1–30 (29); original emphasis.

53. Sugirtharajah, *Postcolonial Criticism and Biblical Interpretation*, 206.

Chapter 3

1. This chapter is closely related to our material published in Stephen Burns, Nicola Slee and Michael N. Jagessar (eds), *The Edge of God: New Liturgical Texts and Contexts in Conversation* (Peterborough: Epworth Press, 2008), 50–66.

2. Dube, "Reading for Decolonization (John 4:1–42)," 56.

3. Charlotte Kroeker (ed.), *Music in Christian Worship* (Collegeville, MN: Liturgical Press, 2005), x.

4. Sugirtharajah, *Postcolonial Reconfigurations*, 4.

5. Hence, while C. Michael Hawn will ask of hymn the following four questions: "What does this song mean for me? What does this song tell me about the God who became human? How does this song help me intercede before God on behalf of the world? How does this song help me welcome the stranger and make more room at the table?," we suggest that postcolonial scrutiny will want to go further to ask questions related to the imperial motives of hymns. (C. Michael Hawn, *Gather into One: Praying and Singing Globally* [Grand Rapids, MI and Cambridge: Eerdmans, 2005], 30).

6. Jeffrey Richards, *Imperialism and Music: Britain 1876–1953* (Manchester: Manchester University Press, 2001).

7. Ian Bradley, *Abide With Me: The World of Victorian Hymns* (London: Bloomsbury Press, 1997), 108.

8. John Hull, "Issac Watts: Experiential Educator to Nationalist Theologian and Hymn Writer," *Panorama: International Congregational Journal of Comparative Religious Education and Values* 14 (2002): 91–106.

9. Methodist Church of Great Britain, *Hymns and Psalms* (Peterborough: Methodist Publishing House, 1983), ix & xii.

10. For example, Gordon Wakefield, *Methodist Spirituality* (Peterborough: Epworth Press, 1999).

11. *Hymns and Psalms* (Methodist Publishing House, 1983), 381.

12. *Hymns and Psalms* (Methodist Publishing House, 1983), 737.

13. *Hymns and Psalms* (Methodist Publishing House, 1983), 719.

14. See Orlando Patterson, *Slavery and Social Death* (Cambridge, MA: Harvard University Press, 1986), 56–58.

15. See Sugirtharajah, *Postcolonial Reconfigurations*, 147.

16. See Richards, *Imperialism and Music*.

17. Bert F. Polman, "Forward Steps and Side Steps in a Walk-Through of Christian Hymnody," in Charlotte Kroeker (ed.), *Music in Christian Worship* (Collegeville, MN: Liturgical Press, 2005), 62–72 (65).

18. As quoted by C. Michael Hawn, "Reverse Missions: Global Singing for Local Congregations," in Charlotte Kroeker (ed.), *Music in Christian Worship* (Collegeville, MN: Liturgical Press, 2005), 98–111 (107).

19. See Said's monumental work, *Orientalism*, which together with Frantz Fanon's writings have greatly influenced postcolonial scholarship.

20. Sugirtharajah, *Postcolonial Reconfigurations*, 148.

21. Sugirtharajah, *Postcolonial Reconfigurations*, 121.

22. Ruth Duck, *Circles of Care: Hymns and Songs* (Cleveland, OH: Pilgrim Press, 1998), ix.

23. Samuel J. Royal makes the observation: "Hymnal editors and editorial committees for compiling hymns do, to an extent, play significant roles in the determination of what hymns will rise to the pews … hymnal editors possess and exercise considerable influence in shaping the definition of the congregational hymn." See essays of Samuel J. Royal, *John Wesley and His Contemporaries: The Texture of the 18th-Century English Culture* (Lampeter: Edwin Mellen Press, 2007), 155.

24. United Church of Christ, *New Century Hymnal* (Cleveland, OH: Pilgrim Press, 1995), x.

25. See Pete Ward, *Growing Up Evangelical* (London: SPCK, 1994), chapter 5, and more recently his *Selling Worship* (Milton Keynes: Paternoster Press, 2005).

26. John Bell, "'Sing a New Song': Interview with Christian Century," *Christian Century* 123/15 (July 25, 2006), 20–23 (20).

27. United Reformed Church, *Rejoice and Sing* (Oxford: Oxford University Press, 1991), v.

28. Inderjeet Parmar, "I am Proud of the British Empire: Why Tony Blair Backs George W. Bush," *The Political Quarterly* (2005): 218–31 (226).

29. Parmar, "I am Proud," 226.

30. *Hymns Ancient & Modern Revised* (Oxford: Oxford University Press, 1981), vi.

31. *Hymns Ancient & Modern Revised*, viii.

32. Sugirtharajah, *Postcolonial Reconfigurations*, 123.

33. Sugirtharajah, *Postcolonial Reconfigurations*, 143.

34. *Common Praise* (Norwich: Canterbury Press, 2000), ix.

35. Sugirtharajah, *Postcolonial Reconfigurations*, 125.

36. Church of Scotland, *Common Ground: A Song Book for All the Churches* (Edinburgh: St. Andrew's Press, 1998), 5.

37. Juan M. C. Oliver, "Just Praise: Prayer Book Revision and Hispanic/ Latino Anglicanism," in Ruth E. Meyers (ed.), *A Prayer Book for the Twenty-first Century* (New York: Church Publishing, 1996), 256–89 (266).

38. See Karen Westerfield Tucker, "A Decade of Christian Song," *Studia Liturgica* 31 (2001): 193–210.

39. Oliver, "Just Praise," 267.

40. Johnsont, "Wanting to be Indian," 281. Our addition in brackets.

41. Hawn, "Reverse Missions," 102–103.

42. R. S. Sugirtharajah, "Introduction," in R. S. Sugirtharajah (ed.), *Vernacular Hermeneutics* (Sheffield: Sheffield Academic Press, 1999), 12.

43. Tucker, "Decade of Christian Song," 206.

44. John D. Witvliet, "The Virtue of Liturgical Discernment," in Charlotte Kroeker (ed.), *Music in Christian Worship* (Collegeville, MN: Liturgical Press, 2005), 83–97 (95).

45. See Brian Wren, *What Language Shall I Borrow? God-talk in Worship: A Male Response to Feminist Theology* (London: SCM Press, 1990).

46. United Church of Christ, *New Century Hymnal*, 880.

47. The hymns of June Boyce-Tillman also provide some important counterpoints. See also her *Unconventional Wisdom* (London: Equinox, 2007).

Chapter 4

1. Joe Aldred, "Paradigms for a Black Theology in Britain," *Black Theology in Britain: A Journal of Contextual Praxis* 2.1 (1999): 9–23 (9).

2. Michael N. Jagessar, *Full Life for All: The Work and Theology of Philip A. Potter. A Historical Survey and Systematic Analysis of Major Themes* (Zotermeer: Bokencentrum, 1997), 110–12.

3. Robert Beckford, *Jesus Dub: Theology, Music and Social Change* (London: Routledge, 2006).

4. Anthony G. Reddie, *Working Against the Grain: Re-imagining Black Theology in the 21st Century* (London: Equinox, 2008).

5. Emmanuel Y. Lartey, *Pastoral Theology in an Intercultural World* (Peterborough: Epworth Press, 2006), 31.

6. Sugirtharajah, "The First, Second and Third Letters of John," 413.

7. Roland Boer, *Rescuing the Bible* (London: Blackwell, 2007), 56–65.

8. R. S. Sugirtharajah, "Postcolonial and Biblical Interpretation: The Next Phase," in Fernando Segovia and R. S. Sugirtharajah (eds), *A Postcolonial Commentary on the New Testament Writings* (London: T&T Clark, 2007), 455–66 (455).

9. Sugirtharajah, "The Next Phase," 456–57.

10. For exploration of the RCL, see Ramshaw, *Treasures Old and New* and Gail Ramshaw, *A Three-Year Banquet: Lectionary for the Assembly* (Minneapolis, MN: Augsburg Press, 2006).

11. See Burns, *Liturgy*, 82–92.

12. Gordon W. Lathrop, "At Least Two Words: The Liturgy as Proclamation," in Blair Gilmore Meeks (ed.), *The Landscape of Praise: Readings in Liturgical Renewal* (Valley Forge, PA: Trinity Press International, 1996), 183–85 (183). On Lathrop's liturgical theology, see Burns, *Worship in Context*, 129–56.

13. See Ramshaw and Lathrop, *Readings for the Assembly*.

14. Lathrop, "At Least Two Words," 183.

15. See his trilogy, *Holy Things: A Liturgical Theology* (Minneapolis, MN: Fortress Press, 1993), *Holy People: A Liturgical Ecclesiology* (Minneapolis, MN: Fortress Press, 1999) and *Holy Ground: A Liturgical Cosmology* (Minneapolis, MN: Fortress Press, 2003) as well as *Central Things: Worship in Word and Sacrament* (Minneapolis, MN: Augsburg Press, 2005).

16. On juxtaposition in the first of Lathrop's trilogy, *Holy Things*, see p. 10 for the first mention of "intentional juxtaposition" and then follow references in the index.

17. This phrase is attributed to Michael Vasey, much used in his speech on the Bible.

18. Michael Vasey, *Strangers and Friends: A New Exploration of Homosexuality and the Bible* (London: Hodder and Stoughton, 1995).

19. Edward Said, *Culture and Imperialism* (London: Vintage Books, 1993).

20. Richard Giles, *Times and Seasons: Creating Transformative Worship Throughout the Year* (Norwich: Canterbury Press, 2008).

21. Richard Giles, *Creating Uncommon Worship: Transforming the Liturgy of the Eucharist*, 3rd edn (Norwich: Canterbury Press, 2004).

22. Giles, *Creating Uncommon Worship*, 234.

23. Giles, *Times and Seasons*, 39–40.

24. *Common Worship: Services and Prayers for the Church of England* (London: Church House Publishing, 2000), 332.

25. *Common Worship: Services*, 540.

26. *Common Worship: Services*, 540. For some worked examples, see Appendix A in Stephen Burns, ed., *Journey* (Norwich: Canterbury Press, 2008).

27. For feminist critique, see Marjorie Procter-Smith, "Feminist Interpretation and Liturgical Proclamation," in Elisabeth Schüssler-Fiorenza (ed.), *Searching the Scriptures: Volume 1: A Feminist Introduction* (London: SCM Press, 1993), 313–25 and Elizabeth J. Smith, *Bearing Fruit in Due Season: Feminist Hermeneutics and the Bible in Worship* (Collegeville, MN: Liturgical Press, 1999).

28. For extended explorations on this theme, see essays in Burns and Monro (eds), *Christian Worship in Australia*.

29. Sugirtharajah, *Postcolonial Criticism and Biblical Interpretation*, 40.

30. Sugirtharajah, "The First, Second and Third Letters of John," 415.

31. Jean Pierre Ruiz, "Taking a Stand on the Seashore: A Postcolonial Exploration of Revelation 13," in David L. Barr, *Reading the Book of Revelation: A Resource for Students* (Atlanta, GA: Society of Biblical Literature, 2003), 119–36 (124).

32. Sugirtharajah, "The Next Phase," 455.

33. Sugirtharajah, "The Next Phase," 465.

34. Citations from Jione Havea, "Local Lectionary Sites," in Stephen Burns and Anita Monro (eds), *Christian Worship in Australia: Inculturating the Liturgical Tradition* (Strathfield, NSW: St Pauls, 2009), 115–26.

35. C. I. David Joy, *Mark and Its Subalterns: A Hermeneutical Paradigm for a Postcolonial Context* (London: Equinox, 2008).

Chapter 5

1. Selby Spong, "Rethinking the Festival of Lessons and Carols," *The Voice* (January 1997), 1. This article was accessed online: http://www.dioceseof-newark.org/vox20197.html

2. Spong, "Rethinking," 3.

3. *Common Worship: Times and Seasons* (London: Church House Publishing, 2006), 88–91.

4. 2005 order accessed online: http://www.kings.cam.ac.uk/chapel/ninelessons/2005/NineLessonsCarols2005.pdf

5. David Isiohro, "Black Theology, Englishness and the Church of England," in Michael N. Jagessar and Anthony G. Reddie (eds), *Postcolonial Black British Theology: New Textures and Themes* (Peterborough: Epworth Press, 2007), 62–67 (63).

6. *Times and Seasons*, 64.

7. http://www.kings.cam.ac.uk/events/chapel-services/nine-lessons.html

8. http://www.kings.cam.ac.uk/events/chapel-services/nine-lessons.html

9. Rudyard Kipling, "The White Man's Burden," *McClure's Magazine* (New York, February 1899). Accessed online. See, for example, http://historymatters.gmu.edu/d/5478/

10. Rudyard Kipling, *Kim* (Scotland: McMillan & Co., 1901).

11. Susan Thorne, *Congregational Missions and the Making of an Imperial Culture in 19th-Century England* (Stanford, CA: Stanford University Press, 1999), 9.

12. E. Said, *Culture and Imperialism* (London: Vintage Books, 1993), 73.

13. Thorne, *Congregational Missions*, 4.

14. J. Cain and A. G. Hopkins, *British Imperialism: Innovation and Expansion 1688–1914* (London: Longman, 1993), 46.

15. Thorne, *Congregational Missions*, 4.

16. Edouard Glissant, *Caribbean Discourse: Selected Essays* (Charlottesville, VA: University Press of Virginia, 1989), 2.

17. Antoinette Burton, "Rules of Thumb: British History and 'Imperial Culture' in Nineteenth and Twentieth-century Britain," *Women's History Review* 3.4 (1994): 483–501 (486).

18. *Times and Seasons*, 88.

19. Referring to "Sovereign" rather than "Lord," as in some feminist practice, might de-gender male terminology, but from a postcolonial perspective, is of little revisionist merit.

20. *Times and Seasons*, 91.

21. *Times and Seasons*, 90.

22. *Times and Seasons*, 90.

23. Janet Wooton, *Introducing a Practical Feminist Theology of Worship* (Sheffield: Sheffield Academic Press, 2000).

24. *Times and Seasons*, 90–1.

25. http://www.kings.cam.ac.uk/events/chapel-services/nine-lessons.html

26. See E. Byron Anderson, "Christian Prayer and Song in a Post-Holocaust Church," *Studies in Christian-Jewish Relations* 1.1 (2005): 104–126.

27. Spong, "Rethinking," 1.

28. Spong, "Rethinking," 1.

29. Clive Pearson (ed.), *Faith in a Hyphen: Cross-Cultural Theologies Down Under* (North Parramatta, NSW: UTC Publications, 2005).

30. Henry F. Knight, *Celebrating Holy Week in a Post-Holocaust World* (Louisville, KY: Westminster John Knox Press, 2005).

31. For example, *Uniting in Worship 2*, the recently published worship book of the Uniting Church of Australia, incorporates a sequence of nine Hebrew scripture portions interspersed with Psalms, followed by one reading from a Christian epistle and a culminating gospel reading. *Evangelical Lutheran Worship*, the recently published worship book of the Evangelical Lutheran Church in America, incorporates a sequence of fourteen readings, twelve from the Hebrew scriptures (some of which may be omitted, but four of which are mandated), with one reading from a Christian epistle and a culminating gospel reading. In both books, the Christian epistle is the baptismal pericope of Romans 6:3-11, and the Lutheran book also includes Psalms – although sometimes other poetic Hebrew texts – as responses. See *Uniting in Worship 2* (Sydney, NSW: Uniting Church Press, 2005), 640–46; *Evangelical Lutheran Worship* (Minneapolis, MN: Augsburg Fortress Press, 2006), 269–70.

32. *Times and Seasons*, 373.

33. *Times and Seasons*, 372.
34. *Times and Seasons*, 372.
35. *Times and Seasons*, 373.
36. *Time and Seasons*, 373.
37. *Time and Seasons*, 382.
38. *Evangelical Lutheran Worship*, 269.
39. *New Century Hymnal*, vii.
40. *New Century Hymnal*, x.
41. *New Century Hymnal*, xi.
42. Burns, *Worship in Context*, 101.
43. See discussion in Part 3.
44. There are a number of such councils with access to publications available online. See for instance: www.refugeecouncil.org.au; www.rcusa.org; www.nrc.no; www.ccrweb.ca
45. See Robert Goss, *Queering Christ: Beyond Jesus Acting Up* (Cleveland, OH: Pilgrim Press, 2002).
46. Jagessar, "Spinning Theology." Gordon W. Lathrop relates Anancy to the Coyote myth of Native American culture in his "*Ordo* and Coyote: Further Reflections on Order, Disorder and Meaning in Christian Worship," *Worship* 80.2 (2006): 194–212, itself based on his "Berakah Response," in Joyce Ann Zimmerman (ed.), *Proceedings of the North American Academy of Liturgy Annual Meeting* (Notre Dame, IN: NAAL, 2006), 26–40.
47. See Isabel Wollaston, "What Can – and Cannot – Be Said," *Journal of Literature and Theology* 6 (1992): 47–56; see also Burns, "Forgiveness in Challenging Circumstances."
48. See http://www.lifewords.info/asylum/reflect/services.html
49. Hoyt Hickman, Don E. Saliers, Laurence Hull Stookey and James F. White, *New Handbook of the Christian Year* (Nashville, TN: Abingdon Press, 1992), 190.
50. One of the things that might be learned in solidarity with the Holocaust literature is Primo Levi's sense of the only hope for the future emerging from insistent emphasis on the apparently negative: see Burns, "Forgiveness in Challenging Circumstances."
51. Don E Saliers, *The Soul in Paraphrase: Prayer and the Religious Affections*, 2nd edn (Akron, OH: OSL Publications, 1991), 80.
52. See Beckford, *Jesus Dub*.
53. Walter Dietrich and Ulrich Luz (eds), *The Bible in a World Context* (Grand Rapids, MI: Eerdmans, 2001). Although increasing numbers of other cross-cultural readings are also now readily available, we accent this one here because of its focus on Christmas narratives.
54. See Sugirtharajah, "Muddling Along at the Margins," 8–21.
55. In the first theory, 25 December is understood to have become the day on which Christians chose to celebrate Jesus' birthday in contest to devotion

to the Unconquered Sun observed by pagans in the society they shared. In choosing this particular date, Christians proclaimed Jesus – understood to be "the sun of righteousness" – as brighter, greater than the deity to whom pagans turned, thereby inviting a new allegiance to Christ. In the second theory, the date of 25 December emerges from creative mathematics related to dating Jesus' crucifixion to March 25, corresponding to Nissan 14, when Passover fell on the year of Jesus' death. In Jewish midrash, greatness was considered to be signalled by having the same calendar date of birth and death, hence heroes of the Jewish faith were believed to be born and to die on the same date of the year. The Christian invention of this tradition was to imagine the date of Jesus' *conception* as corresponding to the date of his death, thereby singling him out above even the greatest figures among the Jewish people. 25 December of course follows 25 March nine months later, hence his "birthday." For further elaboration, see Stephen Burns, "Some Liturgical Perspectives," in Nicola Slee and Rosie Miles (eds), *Doing December Differently: An Alternative Christmas Handbook* (Glasgow: Wild Goose Publications, 2006), 120–23.

Chapter 6

1. David Joy, "Images of Ministry: A Postcolonial Re-Reading," in Michael N. Jagessar and Anthony G. Reddie, *Postcolonial Black British Theology: New Textures and Themes* (Peterborough: Epworth Press, 2007), 51–61 (57).

2. See Fredrica Harris Thompsett, "The Primacy of Baptism: A Reaffirmation of Authority in the Church," in Ian T. Douglas and Kwok Pui-lan (eds), *Beyond Colonial Anglicanism: The Anglican Communion in the Twenty-First Century* (New York: Church Publishing, 2001), 247–69 (251).

3. Barbara Brown Taylor, *Leaving Church: A Memoir of Faith* (San Francisco, CA: HarperCollins, 2006), 119–20.

4. Sugirtharajah, "The First, Second and Third Letters of John," 416.

5. See Elisabeth Schüssler-Fiorenza, *The Power of the Word: Scripture and the Rhetoric of Empire* (Minneapolis, MN: Fortress Press, 2007).

6. See Thompsett, "The Primacy of Baptism," 257.

7. WCC, *Baptism, Eucharist and Ministry*. See http://www.oikoumene. org/resources/documents/wcc-commissions/faith-and-order-commission/ i-unity-the-church-and-its-mission/baptism-eucharist-and-ministry-faith-and-order-paper-no-111-the-lima-text.html

8. Discussion of the Common Worship "affirmation of commitment" draws on material by Stephen Burns published in *An International Journal of Public Theology* 3 (2009): 371–89.

9. The title "affirmation of commitment" is given to this script in 2000, *Common Worship: Services and Prayers for the Church of England* (London: Church House Publishing), 152. See 2006, *Common Worship: Christian Initiation* (London: Church House Publishing), 73. See also, for example, *Common Worship: Services*, 55 and *Common Worship: Daily Prayer* (London: Church House Publishing, 2006), 313.

10. Paul Bradshaw (ed.), *Companion to Common Worship*, vol. 1 (London: SPCK, 2002).

11. Leonel L. Mitchell, *Praying Shapes Believing: A Theological Commentary on the Book of Common Prayer*, 2nd edn (New York: Morehouse, 1991).

12. See Rowan Williams, "Sacraments of a New Society," in David Brown and Ann Loades (eds), *Christ the Sacramental Word: Incarnation, Sacrament and Poetry* (London: SPCK, 1996), 89–102.

13. Rob Bos and Geoff Thompson (eds), *Theology for Pilgrims: Selected Theological Documents from the Uniting Church in Australia* (Sydney: Uniting Church Press, 2008).

14. Bos and Thompson, "Introduction to…" the ministry reports of the 1990s, in Bos and Thompson (eds), *Theology for Pilgrims*, 231.

15. Basis of Union, 14, in Bos and Thompson (eds), *Theology for Pilgrims*, 201.

16. A helpful general resource in this vein is Pui-lan, Compier and Rieger (eds), *Empire and the Christian Tradition*.

17. We need of course to remember the remarkable capacity of the tradition to present internal subversions of itself, and the importance of "searching for lost coins" within it which enable destabilization of sedimented "norms." Tactics can be learned throughout wide sweeps of contemporary theology, a formative influence on me being Ann Loades, *Feminist Theology: Voices from the Past* (Oxford: Polity Press, 2001).

18. See Bos and Thompson (eds), *Theology for Pilgrims*, 187.

19. Rieger, "Christian Theology and Empires," 13.

20. Sugirtharajah, "The Next Phase," 456.

21. Sugirtharajah, "The Next Phase," 456.

22. Don H. Compier, "The Christian Tradition and Empires: A Reader's Guide," in Kwok Pui-lan, Don H. Compier and Joerg Rieger (eds), *Empire and the Christian Tradition: New Readings of Classical Theologians* (Minneapolis, MN: Fortress Press, 2007), 31–45 (35).

23. Sugirtharajah, "The First, Second and Third Letters of John," 414–15.

24. Sugirtharajah, "The Next Phase," 457.

25. Bhabha, *The Location of Culture*, 86.

26. Material in this section draws on a public lecture, "The Beauty of Formation," by Stephen Burns at UTC on February 16, 2009.

27. From the Charge in the Ordination Service: http://www.assembly.
uca.org.au/worship/resources/13-orderingservices/61-deaconordinationin-
duction.html. Note that the same words are addressed to ministers of the
word.

28. Dube, "Curriculum Transformation," 121.

29. Dube, "Curriculum Transformation," 121.

30. Smith-Christopher, "Abolitionist Exegesis," 133.

31. Dube, "Curriculum Transformation," 123.

32. Note that Chris Budden, *Following Jesus in Invaded Space: Doing
Theology on Aboriginal Land* (Eugene, OR: Wipf and Stock, 2009) contains
profound reflections on operative senses of normalcy.

33. Of course, we know that the term "third world" is much debated in
postcolonial theologies.

34. Dube, "Curriculum Transformation," 124.

35. For a profound reflection on why inclusiveness should be regarded as
a spiritual issue, see Saliers, "Towards a Spirituality of Inclusiveness."

36. Burns, *Liturgy.*

37. Lathrop, *Central Things.*

38. Michael N. Jagessar and Stephen Burns, "Fragments of a Postcolonial
Perspective on Christian Worship," *Worship* 80 (2006): 428–52.

39. Burns, *Liturgy,* reviews in *Reviews in Religion and Theology* and *Praxis*
(the newsletter of an English Anglican liturgical network).

40. See Burns, "Presiding Like a Woman."

Conclusion

1. Havea, "Local Lectionary Sites," 121.

2. David Lowenthal, *The Past is a Foreign Country* (Cambridge: Cambridge
University Press, 1985), 5.

3. Talal Asad, "A Comment on Translation, Critique and Subversion," in A
Dingwaney and C. Maier (eds), *Between Languages and Cultures: Translation
and Cross-cultural Texts* (Delhi: Oxford University Press, 1996), 328, cited in
Sugirtharajah, *The Bible and the Third World,* 267.

4. Said, *Culture and Imperialism,* 1.

5. See Gerard Manley Hopkins, *Pied Beauty.* See, for example, http://
www.poetryfoundation.org/archive/poem.html?id=173664

6. Rieger, "Christian Theology and Empires," 13.

7. Reiger, "Christian Theology and Empires," 13.

Bibliography

Aldred, Joe, "Paradigms for a Black Theology in Britain." *Black Theology in Britain: A Journal of Contextual Praxis* 2.1 (1999): 9–23.

Anderson, E. Byron, "Christian Prayer and Song in a Post-Holocaust Church." *Studies in Christian-Jewish Relations* 1.1 (2005): 104–126.

Asad, Talal, "A Comment on Translation, Critique and Subversion." In A. Dingwaney and C. Maier (eds), *Between Languages and Cultures: Translation and Cross-cultural Texts*. Delhi: Oxford University Press, 1996.

Ashcroft, Bill, Gareth Griffiths, and Helen Tiffin, *The Postcolonial Studies Reader*. New York: Routledge, 1995.

Atwell, Robert, *Celebrating the Saints*. Norwich: Canterbury Press, 1998.

Barton, Mukti, "I am Black and Beautiful." *Black Theology: An International Journal* 2.2 (2004): 167–87.

— *Rejection, Resistance, Resurrection: Speaking Out on Racism in the Church*. London: Darton, Longman and Todd, 2005.

Beckford, Robert, *Jesus Dub: Theology, Music and Social Change*. London: Routledge, 2006.

Bell, John, " 'Sing a New Song': Interview with Christian Century." *Christian Century* 123/15 (July 25, 2006): 20–23.

Best, Thomas F. and Dagmar Heller (eds), *Worship Today: Understanding, Practice, Ecumenical Implications*. Geneva: World Council of Churches, 2004.

Bhabha, Homi, *The Location of Culture*. London: Routledge, 1994.

Boer, Roland, *Rescuing the Bible*. London: Blackwell, 2007.

Bos, Rob and Geoff Thompson Thompson (eds), *Theology for Pilgrims: Selected Theological Documents from the Uniting Church in Australia*. Sydney: Uniting Church Press, 2008.

Boyce-Tillman, June, *Unconventional Wisdom*. London: Equinox, 2007.

Bradley, Ian, *Abide With Me: The World of Victorian Hymns*. London: Bloomsbury Press, 1997.

Bradshaw, Paul F., *The Search for the Origins of Christian Worship*. 2nd edn. London: SPCK, 2002.

— *Eucharistic Origins*. London: SPCK, 2004.

Bradshaw, Paul F. (ed.), *Companion to Common Worship*, vol. 1. London: SPCK, 2002.

— *The New SCM Dictionary of Liturgy and Worship*. London: SCM Press, 2002.

Brathwaite, Kamau, "History, the Caribbean Writer, and *X/Self.*" In Geoffrey Davies and Hena Maes-Jelinek (eds), *Crisis and Creativity in the New Literatures in English*, 23–45. Amsterdam: Rodopi, 1990.

Brown, Michelle P., *Christian Art*. London: Lion, 2008.

Brueggemann, Walter, *Texts under Negotiation: The Bible and Postmodern Imagination*. Minneapolis, MN: Fortress Press, 1993.

Bryden, Diana and Helen Tiffin, *Decolonising Fictions*. Denmark: Dangaroo Press, 1993.

Budden, Chris, *Following Jesus in Invaded Space: Doing Theology on Aboriginal Land*. Eugene, OR: Wipf and Stock, 2009.

Burns, Stephen, "Forgiveness in Challenging Circumstances." In Fraser Watts and Elizabeth Gulliford (eds), *Forgiveness in Context: Theology and Psychology in Creative Dialogue*, 144–59. London: Continuum, 2004.

— *Welcoming Asylum Seekers*. Cambridge: Grove Books, 2004.

— *Liturgy*. London: SCM Press, 2006.

— "Some Liturgical Perspectives." In Nicola Slee and Rosie Miles (eds), *Doing December Differently: An Alternative Christmas Handbook*. Glasgow: Wild Goose Publications, 2006.

— *Worship in Context: Liturgical Theology, Children and the City*. Peterborough: Epworth Press, 2006.

— "Presiding Like a Woman: Feminist Gestures for Christian Assembly." *Feminist Theology* 18 (2009): 32–54.

Burns, Stephen and Anita Monro (eds), *Christian Worship in Australia: Inculturating the Liturgical Tradition*. Strathfield, NSW: St Pauls, 2009.

Burns, Stephen, Nicola Slee and Michael N. Jagessar (eds), *The Edge of God: New Liturgical Texts and Contexts in Conversation*. Peterborough: Epworth Press, 2008.

Burton, Antoinette, "Rules of Thumb: British History and 'Imperial Culture' in Nineteenth and Twentieth-century Britain." *Women's History Review* 3.4 (1994): 483–501.

Byron, Gay L., *Symbolic Blackness and Ethnic Difference in Early Christian Literature*. London: Routledge, 2002.

Cain, J. and A. G. Hopkins, *British Imperialism: Innovation and Expansion 1688–1914*. London: Longman, 1993.

Chupungco, Anscar, *Cultural Adaptation of the Liturgy*. New York: Paulist Press, 1982.

— *Liturgies of the Future: The Process and Methods of Inculturation*. Mahwah, NJ: Paulist Press, 1989.

— *Liturgical Inculturation: Sacramentals, Religiosity and Catechesis*. Collegeville, MN: Liturgical Press, 1992.

— "The Theological Principle of Adaptation." In Dwight Vogel (ed.), *Primary Sources of Liturgical Theology: A Reader*, 247–52. Collegeville, MN: Liturgical Press, 2000.

Church of Scotland, *Common Ground: A Song Book for All the Churches*. Edinburgh: St. Andrew's Press, 1998.

Common Praise. Norwich: Canterbury Press, 2000.

Common Worship: Christian Initiation. London: Church House Publishing, 2006.

Common Worship: Daily Prayer. London: Church House Publishing, 2006.

Common Worship: Services and Prayers for the Church of England. London: Church House Publishing, 2000.

Common Worship: Times and Seasons. London: Church House Publishing, 2006.

Compier, Don H., "The Christian Tradition and Empires: A Reader's Guide." In Kwok Pui-lan, Don H. Compier and Joerg Rieger (eds), *Empire and the Christian Tradition: New Readings of Classical Theologians*, 31–45. Minneapolis, MN: Fortress Press, 2007.

de Lima, Glauco S., "Preface." In Ian T. Douglas and Kwok Pui-lan (eds), *Beyond Colonial Anglicanism*, 1–8. New York: Church Publishing, 2001.

Dietrich, Walter and Ulrich Luz (eds), *The Bible in a World Context*. Grand Rapids, MI: Eerdmans, 2001.

Donaldson, Laura and Kwok Pui-lan (eds), *Postcolonialism, Feminism and Religious Discourse*. New York: Routledge, 2002.

Douglas, Ian T. and Kwok Pui-lan (eds), *Beyond Colonial Anglicanism: The Anglican Communion in the Twenty-First Century*. New York: Church Publishing, 2001.

Dube, Musa, *Postcolonial Feminist Interpretation of the Bible*. St. Louis, MO: Chalice Press, 2000.

— "Reading for Decolonization (John 4:1–42)." In Musa Dube and Jeffrey L. Staley (eds), *John and Postcolonialism: Travel, Space and Power*, 51–75. London: Sheffield Academic Press, 2002.

— "Curriculum Transformation: Dreaming of Decolonization in Theological Studies." In D. N. Premnath (ed.), *Border Crossings: Cross-Cultural Hermeneutics. Essays in Honor of R. S. Sugirtharajah*, 121–38. Maryknoll, NY: Orbis Books, 2007.

Duck, Ruth, *Circles of Care: Hymns and Songs*. Cleveland, OH: Pilgrim Press, 1998.

Duraisingh, Christopher, "Towards a Postcolonial Re-Visioning of the Church's Faith, Witness and Communion." In Ian T. Douglas and Kwok Pui-lan (eds), *Beyond Colonial Anglicanism*, 337–67. New York: Church Publishing, 2001.

Eck, Diana, "Prospects for Pluralism: Voice and Vision in the Study of Religion." *Journal of the American Academy of Religion* 75.4 (2007): 743–76.

Evangelical Lutheran Church in America, *Evangelical Lutheran Worship*. Minneapolis, MN: Augsburg Fortress Press, 2006.

Fabella, Virginia and R. S. Sugirtharajah (eds), *The SCM Dictionary of Third World Theologies*. London: SCM Press, 2003.

Fanon, Frantz, *Wretched of the Earth*. New York: Grove Press, 1965.

— *Black Skin, White Masks*. London: Pluto Press, 1986.

Flannery, Austin (ed.), *Vatican Council II: Conciliar and Post-Conciliar Documents*. New York: Costello, 1975.

Ford, David F., *The Shape of Living*. London: Fount, 1997.

Ford, David F., *Self and Salvation: Being Transformed*. Cambridge: Cambridge University Press, 1999.

Ford, David F., *The Modern Theologians*. Oxford: Blackwell, 2005 [1989].

Ford, David F. and Daniel W. Hardy, *Living in Praise: Worshipping and Knowing God*. London: Darton, Longman and Todd, 2005.

Gates, Henry Louis Jr, *The Signifying Monkey: A Theory of Afro-American Literary Criticism*. New York: Oxford University Press, 1988.

Giles, Richard, *Creating Uncommon Worship: Transforming the Liturgy of the Eucharist*. 3rd edn. Norwich: Canterbury Press, 2004.

— *Times and Seasons: Creating Transformative Worship Throughout the Year*. Norwich: Canterbury Press, 2008.

Glissant, Edouard, *Caribbean Discourse: Selected Essays*. Charlottesville, VA: University Press of Virginia, 1989.

Goss, Robert, *Queering Christ: Beyond Jesus Acting Up*. Cleveland, OH: Pilgrim Press, 2002.

Grau, Marion, "Divine Commerce: A Postcolonial Christology of the Times of Neocolonial Empire." In Catherine Keller, Michael Nausner and Mayra Rivera (eds), *Postcolonial Theologies: Divinity and Empire*. St. Louis: MO: Chalice Press, 2004.

— *Of Divine Economy: Refinancing Redemption*. New York: T&T Clark International, 2004.

Hamid, Idris, *In Search of New Perspectives*. Trinidad: CCC, 1972.

Hardy, Daniel W. and David F. Ford, *Jubilate: Theology in Praise*. London: Darton, Longman and Todd, 1984.

Havea, Jione, "Local Lectionary Sites." In Stephen Burns and Anita Monro (eds), *Christian Worship in Australia: Inculturating the Liturgical Tradition*, 115–26. Strathfield, NSW: St Pauls, 2009.

Hawn, C. Michael, *Gather into One: Praying and Singing Globally*. Grand Rapids, MI: Eerdmans: 2005.

— "Reverse Missions: Global Singing for Local Congregations." In Charlotte Kroeker (ed.), *Music in Christian Worship*, 98–111. Collegeville, MN: Liturgical Press, 2005.

Heelas, Paul, Linda Woodhead et al., *The Spiritual Revolution: Why Religion is Giving Way to Spirituality*. Oxford: Blackwell, 2005.

Hickman, Hoyt, Don E. Saliers, Laurence Hull Stookey and James F. White, *New Handbook of the Christian Year*. Nashville, TN: Abingdon Press, 1992.

Hood, Robert, *Begrimed and Black: Christian Traditions on Black and Blackness*. London: Routledge, 1994.

Hull, John M., *In the Beginning There was Darkness: A Blind Person's Conversations with the Bible*. London: SCM Press, 2001.

— "Isaac Watts: Experiential Educator to Nationalist Theologian and Hymn Writer." *Panorama: International Congregational Journal of Comparative Religious Education and Values* 14 (2002): 91–106.

Hymns Ancient & Modern Revised. Oxford: Oxford University Press, 1981.

Iona Community, *The Courage to Say No*. Glasgow: Wild Goose Resources, 1996.

Isiohro, David, "Black Theology, Englishness and the Church of England." In Michael N. Jagessar and Anthony G. Reddie (eds), *Postcolonial Black British Theology: New Textures and Themes*, 62–67. Peterborough: Epworth Press, 2007.

Jagessar, Michael N., *Full Life for All: The Work and Theology of Philip A. Potter. A Historical Survey and Systematic Analysis of Major Themes*. Zotermeer: Bokencentrum, 1997.

— "Navigating the World of 'White Ecumenism': Insights from Philip Potter." *Wereld en Zending* 31.4 (2002): 32–41.

— "Spinning Theology: Trickster, Texts and Theology." In Michael N. Jagessar and Anthony G. Reddie (eds), *Postcolonial Black British Theology: New Textures and Themes*, 124–46. Peterborough: Epworth Press, 2007.

— "The Sacred in Caribbean Literature: A Theological Conversation." In Dawn Llewellyn and Deborah F. Sawyer (eds), *Reading Spiritualities: Constructing and Representing the Sacred*, 27–50. Aldershot: Ashgate, 2008.

Jagessar, Michael N. and Stephen Burns, "Fragments of a Postcolonial Perspective on Christian Worship." *Worship* 80 (2006): 428–52.

— "Liturgical Studies and Christian Worship: The Postcolonial Challenge." *Black Theology: An International Journal* 5 (2007): 39–62.

Jagessar, Michael N. and Anthony G. Reddie (eds), *Black Theology in Britain: A Reader*. London: Equinox, 2007.

— *Postcolonial Black British Theology: New Textures and Themes*. Peterborough: Epworth Press, 2007.

Jasper, R. C. D. and G. J. Cuming (eds), *Prayers of the Eucharist: Early and Reformed*. 3rd edn. Collegeville, MN: Liturgical Press, 1987.

Joh, Wonhee Anne, *Heart of the Cross: A Postcolonial Christology*. Louisville, KY: Westminster John Knox Press, 2006.

Johnsont, Myke, "Wanting to be Indian: When Spiritual Searching Turns into Cultural Theft." In Joanne Pearson (ed.), *Belief Beyond Boundaries:*

WICCA, Celtic Spirituality and the New Age, 277–94. Aldershot: Ashgate, 2005.

Joy, C. I. David, "Images of Ministry: A Postcolonial Re-Reading." In Michael N. Jagessar and Anthony G. Reddie, *Postcolonial Black British Theology: New Textures and Themes*, 51–61. Peterborough: Epworth Press, 2007.

— *Mark and Its Subalterns: A Hermeneutical Paradigm for a Postcolonial Context*. London: Equinox, 2008.

Keller, Catherine, Michael Nausner and Myra Rivera (eds), *Postcolonial Theologies: Divinity and Empire*. St. Louis, MO: Chalice Press, 2004.

Kings, Graham and Geoff Morgan, *Offerings from Kenya to Anglicanism: Liturgical Texts and Contexts including "A Kenyan Service of Holy Communion"*. Alcuin/GROW Joint Liturgical Study 50. Cambridge: Grove Books, 2001.

Kipling, Rudyard, *Kim*. Scotland: McMillan & Co., 1901.

— "The White Man's Burden." *McClure's Magazine*. New York, February 1899. Accessed online: http://faculty.txwes.edu/csmeller/Human-Prospect/ProData09/01ModCulMatrix/ModWRTs/Kipling1865/Kip1899Burden.htm

Knight, Henry F., *Celebrating Holy Week in a Post-Holocaust World*. Louisville, KY: Westminster John Knox Press, 2005.

Kroeker, Charlotte (ed.), *Music in Christian Worship*. Collegeville, MN: Liturgical Press, 2005.

Kwok, Pui-lan "The Legacy of Cultural Hegemony in the Anglican Church." In Ian T. Douglas and Kwok Pui-lan (eds), *Beyond Colonial Anglicanism: The Anglican Communion in the Twenty-First Century*, 47–70. New York: Church Publishing, 2001.

— *Postcolonial Imagination and Feminist Theology*. London: SCM Press, 2005.

— "Theology and Social Theory." In Kwok Pui-lan, Don H. Compier and Joerg Rieger (eds), *Empire and the Christian Tradition: New Readings of Classical Theologians*, 15–29. Minneapolis, MN: Fortress Press, 2007.

Kwok, Pui-lan, Don H. Compier and Joerg Rieger (eds), *Empire and the Christian Tradition: New Readings of Classical Theologians*. Minneapolis, MN: Fortress Press, 2007.

Lartey, Emmanuel, *In Living Colour: An Intercultural Approach to Pastoral Care and Counselling*. London: Cassell, 1997.

— *Pastoral Theology in an Intercultural World*. Peterborough: Epworth Press, 2006.

Lathrop, Gordon W., *Holy Things: A Liturgical Theology*. Minneapolis, MN: Fortress Press, 1993.

— "At Least Two Words: The Liturgy as Proclamation." In Blair Gilmore Meeks (ed.), *The Landscape of Praise: Readings in Liturgical Renewal*, 183–85. Valley Forge, PA: Trinity Press International, 1996.

— *Holy People: A Liturgical Ecclesiology.* Minneapolis, MN: Fortress Press, 1999.

— *Holy Ground: A Liturgical Cosmology.* Minneapolis, MN: Fortress Press, 2003.

— *Central Things: Worship in Word and Sacrament.* Minneapolis, MN: Augsburg Press, 2005.

— "Berakah Response." In Joyce Ann Zimmerman (ed.), *Proceedings of the North American Academy of Liturgy Annual Meeting,* 26–40. Notre Dame, IN: NAAL, 2006.

— "*Ordo* and Coyote: Further Reflections on Order, Disorder and Meaning in Christian Worship." *Worship* 80.2 (2006): 194–212.

Leone, Massimo, *Religious Conversion and Identity: The Semiotic Analysis of Texts.* London: Routledge, 2004.

Loades, Ann, *Searching for Lost Coins.* London: SPCK, 1987.

— *Feminist Theology: Voices from the Past.* Oxford: Polity Press, 2001.

Long, Charles, *Significations: Signs, Symbols, and Images in the Interpretation of Religion.* Philadelphia, PA: Fortress Press, 1986.

Lowenthal, David, *The Past is a Foreign Country.* Cambridge: Cambridge University Press, 1985.

Methodist Church of Great Britain, *Hymns and Psalms.* Peterborough: Methodist Publishing House, 1983.

— *Methodist Worship Book.* Peterborough: Methodist Publishing House, 1999.

Mitchell, Leonel L., *Praying Shapes Believing: A Theological Commentary on the Book of Common Prayer.* 2nd edn. New York: Morehouse, 1991.

Oliver, Juan M. C., "Just Praise: Prayer Book Revision and Hispanic/Latino Anglicanism." In Ruth E. Meyers (ed.), *A Prayer Book for the Twenty-first Century,* 256–89. New York: Church Publishing, 1996.

Parmar, Inderjeet, "I am Proud of the British Empire: Why Tony Blair Backs George W. Bush." *The Political Quarterly* (2005): 218–31.

Patterson, Orlando, *Slavery and Social Death.* Cambridge, MA: Harvard University Press, 1986.

Pearson, Clive (ed.), *Faith in a Hyphen: Cross-Cultural Theologies Down Under.* North Parramatta, NSW: UTC Publications, 2005.

Philippart, David, *Saving Signs, Wondrous Words.* Chicago: Liturgy Training Publications, 1996.

Polman, Bert F., "Forward Steps and Side Steps in a Walk-Through of Christian Hymnody." In Charlotte Kroeker (ed.), *Music in Christian Worship,* 62–72. Collegeville, MN: Liturgical Press, 2005.

Procter-Smith, Marjorie, "Feminist Interpretation and Liturgical Proclamation." In Elisabeth Schüssler-Fiorenza (ed.), *Searching the Scriptures: Volume 1: A Feminist Introduction,* 313–25. London: SCM Press, 1993.

Ramshaw, Gail, *Worship: Searching for Language*. Washington DC: Pastoral Press, 1988.
— *God Beyond Gender: Feminist Christian God-Language*. Minneapolis, MN: Fortress Press, 1995.
— *Liturgical Language: Making it Metaphoric, Keeping it Inclusive*. Collegeville, MN: Liturgical Press, 1996.
— *Under the Tree of Life: The Religion of a Feminist Christian*. New York: Continuum, 1999.
— *Reviving Sacred Speech: The Meaning of Liturgical Language*. 2nd edn. Akron, OH: OSL Publications, 2000.
— *Treasures Old and New: Images in the Lectionary*. Minneapolis, MN: Fortress Press, 2002.
— *A Three-Year Banquet: Lectionary for the Assembly*. Minneapolis, MN: Augsburg Press, 2006.
Ramshaw, Gail, and Gordon W. Lathrop (eds), *Readings for the Assembly*, cycles A, B and C. 3 vols. Minneapolis, MN: Fortress Press, 1995–97.
Reddie, Anthony G., *Nobodies to Somebodies: A Practical Theology for Education and Liberation*. Peterborough: Epworth Press, 2003.
— *Working Against the Grain: Re-imagining Black Theology in the 21st Century*. London: Equinox, 2008.
Richards, Jeffrey, *Imperialism and Music: Britain 1876–1953*. Manchester: Manchester University Press, 2001.
Rieger, Joerg, "Christian Theology and Empires." In Kwok Pui-lan, Don H. Compier and Joerg Rieger (eds), *Empire and the Christian Tradition: New Readings of Classical Theologians*, 1–13. Minneapolis, MN: Fortress Press, 2007.
— *Christ and Empire: From Paul to Postcolonial Times*. Minneapolis, MN: Fortress Press, 2007.
Rivera, Mayra, *The Touch of Transcendence: A Postcolonial Theology of God*. Louisville, KY: Westminster John Knox Press, 2007.
Royal, Samuel J., *John Wesley and His Contemporaries: The Texture of the 18th-Century English Culture*. Lampeter: Edwin Mellen Press, 2007.
Ruiz, Jean Pierre, "Taking a Stand on the Seashore: A Postcolonial Exploration of Revelation 13." In David L. Barr, *Reading the Book of Revelation: A Resource for Students*, 119–36. Atlanta, GA: Society of Biblical Literature, 2003.
Said, Edward, *Orientalism: Western Representations of the Orient*. London: Routledge, 1978.
— *Culture and Imperialism*. London: Vintage Books, 1993.
Saliers, Don E., *The Soul in Paraphrase: Prayer and the Religious Affections*. 2nd edn. Akron, OH: OSL Publications, 1991.

— "Towards a Spirituality of Inclusiveness." In Nancy Eisland and Don E. Saliers (eds), *Human Disability and the Service of God: Reassessing Religious Practice*, 1–30. Nashville, TN: Abingdon Press, 1998.

Schaper, Donna E., *Raising Interfaith Children: Spiritual Orphans or Spiritual Heirs?* New York: Crossroad, 1999.

Schüssler-Fiorenza, Elisabeth, *The Power of the Word: Scripture and the Rhetoric of Empire*. Minneapolis, MN: Fortress Press, 2007.

Segovia, Fernando F., *Interpreting Beyond Borders*. London: Sheffield Academic Press, 2000.

— "Mapping the Postcolonial Optic in Biblical Criticism: Meaning and Scope." In Stephen C. Moore and Fernando F. Segovia (eds), *Postcolonial Biblical Criticism: Interdisciplinary Intersections*, 23–78. London: T&T Clark, 2005.

Shanti, Margaret, "Worship/Rituals." In Virginia Fabella and R. S. Sugirtharajah Sugirtharajah (eds), *The SCM Dictionary of Third World Theologies*. London: SCM Press, 2003.

Smith, Elizabeth J., *Bearing Fruit in Due Season: Feminist Hermeneutics and the Bible in Worship*. Collegeville, MN: Liturgical Press, 1999.

Smith-Christopher, Daniel, "Abolitionist Exegesis: A Quaker Proposal for White Liberals." In R. S. Sugitharajah (ed.), *Still at the Margins: Biblical Scholarship Fifteen Years after Voices from the Margins*, 128–38. London: T&T Clark, 2008.

Snell, Donald, "Rending the Temple Veil: Holy Space in Holy Community." In John Ander Runckle (ed.), *Searching for Sacred Space: Essays on Architecture and Liturgical Design in the Episcopal Church*, 149–81. New York: Church Publishing, 2002.

Spivak, Gayatri Chakravorty, "Can the Subaltern Speak?" In Cary Nelson and Lawrence Grossberg (eds), *Marxism and the Interpretation of Culture*, 271–313. Urbana, IL: University of Illinois Press, 1988.

Spong, Selby, "Rethinking the Festival of Lessons and Carols." *The Voice* (January 1997), http://www.dioceseofnewark.org/vox20197.html.

Staley, Jeffrey L., "'Dis Place Man': A PostcolonialPostcolonial Critique of the Vine (the Mountain and the Temple) in the Gospel of John." In Musa Dube and Jeffrey L. Staley (eds), *John and Postcolonialism: Travel, Space and Power*, 32–50. London: Sheffield Academic Press, 2002.

Sugirtharajah, R. S., *The Bible and the Third World: Precolonial, Colonial and Postcolonial Encounters*. Cambridge: Cambridge University Press, 2001.

— *Postcolonial Criticism and Biblical Interpretation*. Oxford: Oxford University Press, 2002.

— *Postcolonial Reconfigurations: An Alternative Way of Reading the Bible and Doing Theology*. London: SCM Press, 2003.

— "Postcolonial Biblical Interpretation: The Next Phase." In R. S. Sugirtharajah (ed.), *A Postcolonial Commentary on the New Testament*, 455–66. London: T&T Clark, 2005.

— *The Postcolonial Biblical Reader*. Oxford: Blackwell, 2006.

— "The First, Second and Third Letters of John." In R. S. Sugirtharajah (ed.), *A Postcolonial Commentary on the New Testament Writings*, 413–23. London: T&T Clark, 2007.

— "Postcolonial and Biblical Interpretation: The Next Phase." In Fernando Segovia and R. S. Sugirtharajah (eds), *A Postcolonial Commentary on the New Testament Writings*, 455–66. London: T&T Clark, 2007.

— "Muddling Along at the Margins." In R. S. Sugitharajah (ed.), *Still at the Margins: Biblical Scholarship Fifteen Years after Voices from the Margins*, 8–21. London: T&T Clark, 2008.

Sugirtharajah, R. S. (ed.), *The Postcolonial Bible*. London: Sheffield Academic Press, 1998

— *Vernacular Hermeneutics*. Sheffield: Sheffield Academic Press, 1999.

Taylor, Barbara Brown, *Leaving Church: A Memoir of Faith*. San Francisco, CA: HarperCollins, 2006.

Thompsett, Fredrica Harris, "The Primacy of Baptism: A Reaffirmation of Authority in the Church." In Ian T. Douglas and Kwok Pui-lan (eds), *Beyond Colonial Anglicanism: The Anglican Communion in the Twenty-First Century*, 247–69. New York: Church Publishing, 2001.

Thorne, Susan, *Congregational Missions and the Making of an Imperial Culture in 19th-Century England*. Stanford, CA: Stanford University Press, 1999.

Tovey, Philip, *Inculturation of Christian Worship: Exploring the Eucharist*. Aldershot: Ashgate, 2004.

Tucker, Karen Westerfield, "A Decade of Christian Song." *Studia Liturgica* 31 (2001): 193–210.

United Church of Christ, *New Century Hymnal*. Cleveland, OH: Pilgrim Press, 1995.

United Reformed Church, *Rejoice and Sing*. Oxford: Oxford University Press, 1991.

Uniting Church of Australia, *Uniting in Worship 2*. Sydney, NSW: Uniting Church Press, 2005.

Vasey, Michael, *Strangers and Friends: A New Exploration of Homosexuality and the Bible*. London: Hodder and Stoughton, 1995.

Vogel, Dwight W. (ed.), *Primary Sources in Liturgical Theology: A Reader*. Collegeville, MN: Liturgical Press, 2000.

Wainwright, Geoffrey, *Worship With One Accord: Where Liturgy and Ecumenism Embrace*. Oxford: Oxford University Press, 1997.

Wakefield, Gordon, *Methodist Spirituality*. Peterborough: Epworth Press, 1999.

Walcott, Derek, "The Sea is History." In *Collected Poems 1948–1984*, 364–67. London: Faber & Faber, 1986.

Walton, Janet, *Feminist Liturgy: A Matter of Justice*. Collegeville, MN: Liturgical Press, 2000.

Ward, Pete, *Growing Up Evangelical*. London: SPCK, 1994.

— *Selling Worship*. Milton Keynes: Paternoster Press, 2005.

Watson, Natalie K. and Stephen Burns (eds), *Exchanges of Grace: Essays in Honour of Ann Loades*. London: SCM Press, 2008.

White, James F., *Protestant Worship: Traditions in Transition*. Louisville, KY: Westminster John Knox Press, 1989.

— *Roman Catholic Worship: From Trent to Today*. Mahwah, NJ: Paulist Press, 1995.

— "Protestant Public Worship in America, 1935–1995." In *Christian Worship in North America: A Retrospective, 1955–1995*, 115–33. Collegeville, MN: Liturgical Press, 1997.

— "How Do We Know it is Us?" In E. Byron Anderson and Bruce Morrill (eds), *Liturgy and the Moral Self: Humanity at Full Stretch Before God*, 55–66. Collegeville, MN: Liturgical Press, 1998.

Williams, Dolores S., *Sisters in the Wilderness: The Challenge of Womanist God-talk*. Maryknoll, NY: Orbis Books, 1993.

Williams, Rowan, "Sacraments of a New Society." In David Brown and Ann Loades (eds), *Christ the Sacramental Word: Incarnation, Sacrament and Poetry*, 89–102. London: SPCK, 1996.

Witvliet, John D., "The Virtue of Liturgical Discernment." In Charlotte Kroeker (ed.), *Music in Christian Worship*, 83–97. Collegeville, MN: Liturgical Press, 2005.

Wollaston, Isabel, "What Can – and Cannot – Be Said." *Journal of Literature and Theology* 6 (1992): 47–56.

Wooton, Janet, *Introducing a Practical Feminist Theology of Worship*. Sheffield: Sheffield Academic Press, 2000.

Wren, Brian, *What Language Shall I Borrow? God-talk in Worship: A Male Response to Feminist Theology*. London: SCM Press, 1990.

Online sources cited/consulted

Http://www.assembly.uca.org.au/worship/resources/13-orderingservices/61-deaconordinationinduction.html

Http://www.kings.cam.ac.uk/events/chapel-services/nine-lessons.html

Http://www.lifewords.info/asylum/reflect/services.html

Http://www.refugeecouncil.org.au

Http://www.rcusa.org

Http://www.nrc.no

Http://www.ccrweb.ca

Index of Names

Index of Subjects

Printed in Great Britain
by Amazon

43130234R00108